SISTER OUTSIDER

Also by Audre Lorde:

The First Cities
Cables to Rage
From a Land Where Other People Live
New York Head Shop and Museum
Between Our Selves
Coal
The Black Unicorn
Use of the Erotic: The Erotic as Power
The Cancer Journals
Chosen Poems: Old and New
Zami: A New Spelling of My Name

SISTER OUTSIDER

Essays and Speeches

by

Audre Lorde

CROSSING PRESS
Berkeley

Acknowledgments

I wish to acknowledge the invaluable help of each one of the women who supported me through these writings, with particular note of appreciation for the patience and insight of my editor, Nancy K. Boreano, who has helped to make the whole process real again.

Text © 1984, 2007 by Audre Lorde

All rights reserved. Published in the United States by Ten Speed Press, an imprint of the Crown Publishing Group, a division of Random House, Inc., New York.
www.crownpublishing.com
www.tenspeed.com

Crossing Press and the Crossing Press colophon are registered trademarks of Random House, Inc.

Library of Congress Cataloging-in-Publication Data

Lorde, Audre.
    Sister outsider.
    (The Crossing Press feminist series)
    I. Title. II. Series.
  PS3562.'75S5   1984   814'.54   84-1844

ISBN-13: 978-1-58091-186-3
ISBN-10: 1-58091-186-2

Printed in the U.S.A.

Cover design by Betsy Stromberg
Cover illustration by Image Club/Getty Images

17 16 15 14 13

Revised Edition

Contents

Foreword

WITH ITS PARADOXICAL TITLE, *Sister Outsider*, Audre Lorde's most influential book of prose, is ever more trenchant twenty-three years after its first printing—surpassing even the reputation of her poetry, which is no minor feat. Were she here among us in the funky U.S. instead of floating somewhere over the Guinea Coast, Lorde would still want and have to claim that "outsider" stance. These prose works, much like her poetry, position her (and us), as Akasha Gloria Hull said many years ago, "on the line," refusing the safety of that inside perimeter. I return to these texts again and always—in these times of imperial and unnatural acts, like the war in Iraq and the federal abandonment of the Gulf Coast survivors in the wake of Hurricane Katrina. *Sister* is my sister no matter how I may reject her counsel: "As Black people . . . we must move against not only those forces which dehumanize us from the outside, but also against those oppressive values which we have been forced to take into ourselves."[1] No matter how angry *Sister* makes me with her seemingly easy aphorisms: "*For the master's tools will never dismantle the master's house.*"[2] No matter how much *Sister* still asks the hard questions: "Why do Black women reserve a particular voice of fury and disappointment for each other? Who is it we must destroy when we attack each other with that tone of predetermined and correct annihilation?"[3]

On the shelf with or at the bottom of that stack of other well-mined tomes—*The Black Woman: An Anthology*; *Conditions: Five, The Black Women's Issue*; *Lesbian Fiction*; *Top Ranking*—*Sister* is never far from me. I retain several dog-eared, underlined, coffee-splotched copies of her—at home, at work, on my nightstand—as necessary as my eyeglasses, my second sight.

A fall semester of teaching my women's studies seminar never passes without deploying one of the following texts in theorizing feminist activism: "Age, Race, Class, and Sex: Women Redefining Difference," "An Open Letter to Mary Daly," or "The Uses of Anger: Women

Responding to Racism." In one paragraph, Lorde can simultaneously blow away the entire Enlightenment project and use its tools, too.

In 1990 I quoted myself in "Knowing the Danger and Going There Anyway," an article I wrote on Lorde for the Boston feminist newspaper, *Sojourner*; I'll change the sister trope and quote myself again: "I said that Audre Lorde's work is 'a neighbor I've grown up with, who can always be counted on for honest talk, to rescue me when I've forgotten the key to my own house, to go with me to a tenants' or town meeting, a community festival'."[4] In 1990, Lorde was still walking among us. *Sister Outsider* has taken its creator's place as that good neighbor. And with this new edition, we will have our good neighbor and sister for another generation. May those of us who are *Sister Outsider*'s old neighbors continue to be inspired by her luminous writing and may those new neighbors be newly inspired.

—CHERYL CLARKE
2007

Notes

1. "Learning from the 60s," p. 135.
2. "The Master's Tools Will Never Dismantle the Master's House," p. 112.
3. "Eye to Eye: Black Women, Hatred, and Anger," p. 159.
4. Cheryl Clarke, *The Days of Good Looks: Prose and Poetry, 1980–2005* (New York: Carroll & Graf, 2006).

Introduction

WHEN WE BEGAN EDITING *Sister Outsider*—long after the book had been conceptualized, a contract signed, and new material written—Audre Lorde informed me, as we were working one afternoon, that she doesn't write theory. "I am a poet," she said.

Lorde's stature as a poet is undeniable. And yet there can be no doubt that *Sister Outsider*, a collection of essays and speeches drawn from the past eight years of this Black lesbian feminist's nonfiction prose, makes absolutely clear to many what some already knew: Audre Lorde's voice is central to the development of contemporary feminist theory. She is at the cutting edge of consciousness.

The fifteen selections included here, several of them published for the first time, are essential reading. Whether it is the by now familiar "Uses of the Erotic: The Erotic as Power," opening us up to the potential power in all aspects of our lives implicit in the erotic,

> When I speak of the erotic, then, I speak of it as an assertion of the life-force of women; of that creative energy empowered, the knowledge and use of which we are now reclaiming in our language, our history, our dancing, our loving, our work, our lives.[1]

or the recently authored "Eye to Eye: Black Women, Hatred, and Anger," probing the white racist roots of hostility between Black women,

> We are Black women born into a society of entrenched loathing and contempt for whatever is Black and female. We are strong and enduring. We are also deeply scarred.[2]

Lorde's work expands, deepens, and enriches all of our understandings of what feminism can be.

But what about the "conflict" between poetry and theory, between their separate and seemingly incompatible spheres? We have been told that poetry expresses what we feel, and theory states what we know; that the poet creates out of the heat of the moment, while the theorist's mode is, of necessity, cool and reasoned; that one is art and therefore experienced "subjectively," and the other is scholarship, held accountable in the "objective" world of ideas. We have been told that poetry has a soul and theory has a mind and that we have to choose between them.

The white western patriarchal ordering of things requires that we believe there is an inherent conflict between what we feel and what we think—between poetry and theory. We are easier to control when one part of our selves is split from another, fragmented, off balance. There are other configurations, however, other ways of experiencing the world, though they are often difficult to name. We can sense them and seek their articulation. Because it is the work of feminism to make connections, to heal unnecessary divisions, *Sister Outsider* is a reason for hope.

Audre Lorde's writing is an impulse toward wholeness. What she says and how she says it engages us both emotionally and intellectually. She writes from the particulars of who she is: Black woman, lesbian, feminist, mother of two children, daughter of Grenadian immigrants, educator, cancer survivor, activist. She creates material from the dailiness of her life that we can use to help shape ours. Out of her desire for wholeness, her need to encompass and address all the parts of herself, she teaches us about the significance of *difference*—"that raw and powerful connection from which our personal power is forged."[3]

A white Jewish lesbian mother, I first read "Man Child: A Black Lesbian Feminist's Response" several years ago as I was struggling to accept the inevitability of my prepubescent son's eventual manhood. Not only would this boy of mine become a man physically, but he might act like one. This awareness turned into a major crisis for me at a time and place when virtually all the lesbian mothers I knew (who I realized, with hindsight, were also white) either insisted that their "androgynous" male children would stay that way, would not grow up to be sexist/misogynist men, or were pressured to choose between a separatist vision of community and their sons. I felt trapped by a narrow range of options.

Lorde, however, had wider vision. She started with the reality of her child's approaching manhood ("Our sons will not grown into women"[4]) and then asked what kind of man he would become. She saw clearly that she could both love her son fiercely *and* let him go. In fact, for their mutual survival, she had no choice but to let him go, to teach him that she "did not exist to do his feeling for him."[5]

Lorde and I are both lesbian mothers who have had to teach our boys to do their own emotional work. But her son Jonathan is Black and my son Joshua is white and that is not a trivial difference in a racist society, despite their common manhood. As Lorde has written elsewhere:

> Some problems we share as women, some we do not. You fear your children will grow up to join the patriarchy and testify against you; we fear our children will be dragged from a car and shot down in the street, and you will turn your backs upon the reasons they are dying.[6]

I read "Man Child," and it was one of those occasions when I can remember something major shifting inside me.

I came to understand it was not merely that Lorde knew more about raising sons than I did, although I had been given expert advice. I realized how directly Lorde's knowledge was tied to her difference—those realities of Blackness and lesbianism that placed her outside the dominant society. She had information that I, a white woman who had lived most of my life in a middle-class heterosexual world, did not have, information I could use, information I needed.

> For in order to survive, those of us for whom oppression is as american as apple pie have always had to be watchers . . . [7]

I was ashamed by my arrogance, frightened that my ignorance would be exposed, and ultimately excited by the possibilities becoming available to me. I made a promise to my future to try and listen to those voices, in others and in myself, that knew what they knew precisely because they were different. I wanted to hear what they had to tell me.

Of course, the reverberations continue.

When I read "Man Child" again several years later, having done a lot of work reclaiming my Jewish identity in the interim, I thought about the complexities of my son being a white Jewish man in a white Christian society. I had not seen this as an issue the first time around; it is hard now to reconstruct my shortsightedness.

> When we define ourselves, when I define myself, the place in which
> I am like you and the place in which I am not like you, I'm not
> excluding you from the joining—I'm broadening the joining.[8]

There is a further reduction of the distance between feeling and
thinking as we become aware of Lorde's internal process. We watch
her move from "the chaos of knowledge . . . that dark and true depth
within each of us that nurtures vision"[9] to "the heretical actions that
our dreams imply."[10] Understanding—the figuring out and piecing
together, the moving from one place to the next, provides the
connections.

> What understanding begins to do is to make knowledge available
> for use, and that's the urgency, that's the push, that's the drive.[11]

Movement is intentional and life-sustaining.

Nowhere is this intentionality more evident than in "The Transformation of Silence into Language and Action." Here Lorde grapples with
a possible diagnosis of cancer. "I had the feeling, probably a body sense,
that life was never going to be the same. . . ."[12] She deals in public, at
an academic gathering, in front of 700 women. She tells us that she is
afraid but that silence is not a protection.

> And it [speaking] is never without fear; of visibility, of the harsh
> light of scrutiny and perhaps judgment, of pain, of death. But we
> have lived through all of those already, in silence, except death.
> And I remind myself all the time now, that if I were to have been
> born mute, and had maintained an oath of silence my whole life
> for safety, I would still have suffered, and I would still die. It is very
> good for establishing perspective.[13]

Lorde's commitment to confront the worst so that she is freed to
experience the best is unshakeable. Although *Sister Outsider* spans
almost a decade of her work, nine of the fifteen pieces in this book
were written in the two years following Lorde's discovery that she
might have/did have cancer. In the process of her growth, her coming
to terms and using what she has learned, she shows us things we
can take with us in our struggles for survival, no matter what our
particular "worst" may be.

> What is there possibly left for us to be afraid of, after we have dealt face to face with death and not embraced it? Once I accept the existence of dying as a life process, who can ever have power over me again?[14]

Audre Lorde asks no more of us than she does of herself: that we pay attention to those voices we have been taught to distrust, that we articulate what they teach us, that we act upon what we know. Just as she develops themes, reworking and building on them over time to create theory, so, too, can we integrate the material of our lives.

Black woman, lesbian, feminist, mother of two children, daughter of Grenadian immigrants, educator, cancer survivor, activist. The essays and speeches in *Sister Outsider* give new resonance to that fundamental but much abused feminist revelation that the personal is political. We are all amplified by Audre Lorde's work.

> I am who I am, doing what I came to do, acting upon you like a drug or a chisel to remind you of your me-ness, as I discover you in myself.[15]

—NANCY K. BEREANO
December 1983

Notes

1. "Uses of the Erotic: The Erotic as Power," p. 55.
2. "Eye to Eye: Black Women, Hatred, and Anger," p. 151.
3. "The Master's Tools Will Never Dismantle the Master's House," p. 112.
4. "Man Child: A Black Lesbian Feminist's Response," p. 73.
5. Ibid., p. 74.
6. "Age, Race, Class, and Sex: Women Redefining Difference," p. 119.
7. Ibid., p. 114.
8. From an interview in *The Feminist Renaissance*.
9. "An Interview: Audre Lorde and Adrienne Rich," p. 100, and "An Open Letter to Mary Daly," p. 68.
10. "Poetry Is Not a Luxury," p. 38.
11. "An Interview," p. 109.
12. Ibid., pp. 108–109.
13. "The Transformation of Silence into Language and Action," p. 43.
14. *The Cancer Journals* (Aunt Lute Books, 1980), p. 25.
15. "Eye to Eye," p. 147.

Notes from a Trip to Russia*

SINCE I'VE RETURNED from Russia a few weeks ago, I've been dreaming a lot. At first I dreamt about Moscow every night. Sometimes my lover and I had returned there; sometimes I would be in warmer, familiar places I had visited; sometimes in different, unfamiliar cities, cold, white, strange. In one dream, I was making love to a woman behind a stack of clothing in Gumm's Department Store in Moscow. She was ill, and we went upstairs, where I said to a matron, "We have to get her to the hospital." The matron said, "All right, you take her over there and tell them that she needs a kidney scan and a brain scan . . . " And I said, "No, they're not going to do that for me." And she looked at me very strangely and she said, "Of course they will." And I realized I was in Russia, and medicine and doctor bills and all the rest of that are free.

My dreams don't come every night anymore, but it seems as if they've gotten deeper and deeper so that I awake not really knowing any of the content of them but only knowing that I've just dreamt about Russia again. For a while, in my dreams, Russia became a mythic representation of that socialism which does not yet exist anywhere I have been. The possibilities of liv-

---

* These are edited journal entries from a two-week trip to Russia that I made in 1976 as the invited American observer to the African-Asian Writers Conference sponsored by the Union of Soviet Writers.

ing in Russia seem very different in some respects, yet the people feel so Western European (so American, really) outside of Tashkent. And the afternoons in Moscow are so dark and gloomy.

I

The flight to Moscow was nine hours long, and from my observations on the plane, Russians are generally as unfriendly to each other as Americans are and just about as unhelpful.

There was a marvelously craggy-faced old blue-eyed woman in her seventies wearing a babushka, with a huge coat roll. On the plane everyone had one kind of huge coat roll or another except me. When I stepped out into the Moscow weather I realized why. But this woman was sitting in the seat right in front of me. She was traveling alone and was too short to wield her roll easily. She tried once, and she tried twice, and finally I got up and helped her. The plane was packed: I'd never seen a plane quite so crowded before. The old woman turned around and looked at me. It was obvious she did not speak English because I had muttered something to her with no reply. There was in her eyes a look of absolutely no rancor. I thought with a quick shock how a certain tension in glances between American Black and white people is taken for granted. There was no thank you either, but there was a kind of simple human response to who I was. And then as she turned to sit back down, under her very dowdy cardigan I saw on her undersweater at least three military-type medals, complete with chevrons. Hero of the Republic medals, I learned later. Earned for hard work.

This is something that I noticed all over: the very old people in Russia have a stamp upon them that I hope I can learn and never lose, a matter-of-fact resilience and sense of their place upon the earth that is very sturdy and reassuring.

I landed on September 10th about 3:30 P.M. Moscow time and stepped out into a very raw, familiar greyness. There was a winter smell to the air; almost nostalgic. The trees were

Thanksgiving-turned and the sky had that turkey-laden grey-pumpkin color. I saw three large, square-faced women arm-in-arm, marching across the airfield laughing and joking as they came. They were evidently workers just going off shift — they had grey coveralls and jackets with engineer caps and carried lunch buckets. They stopped beside a truck that had paused and started beating against the closed window, drawing the attention of the other woman inside with some half-hello/half-joke at the driver, who was obviously their buddy, because they all pointed fingers at each other laughing uproariously together there on the Moscow airstrip in the grim light, swinging their lunch pails and cutting up.

My Intourist guide's name was Helen, a very pleasant and attractive large-boned young woman in her thirties. She was born in the East, near Japan, and her father, who'd been a military man, was dead. She lived with her mother now, and she said that she and her mother had to learn to do a lot of things for themselves since there are so few men around these days and service is so hard to get.

In Russia you carry your own bags in airports and hotels. This, at first, struck me as oppressive because, of course, carrying a laden bag up seven flights of stairs when the elevator isn't working is not fun. But the longer I stayed there the fairer it seemed, because in this country it appears that everything is seen in terms of food. That is, the labor of one's hands is measured by how much food you can produce, and then you take that and compare its importance to the worth of the other work that you do. Some men and women spend their whole lives, for instance, learning and doing the infinitely slow and patient handwork of retouching Persian Blue tiles down in Samarkand to restore the ancient mausoleums. It is considered very precious work. But antiquities have a particular value, whereas carrying someone else's bag does not have a very high priority because it is not very productive either of beauty or worth. If you can't manage it, then that's another story. I find it a very interesting concept.

It's about thirty miles from the airport to the city of Moscow, and the road and the trees and the drivers could have been people from Northern Westchester in late winter, except I couldn't read any of the signs. We would pass from time to time incredibly beautiful, old, uncared for Russian-Orthodox-style houses, with gorgeous painted wooden colors and outlined ornate windows. Some of them were almost falling down. But there was a large ornate richness about the landscape and architecture on the outskirts of Moscow, even in its grey winter, that seemed to tell me immediately that I was not at home.

I stayed at the Hotel Younnost, which is one of the international hotels in Moscow. The room was a square studio affair with Hollywood bed couches, and a huge picture window looking towards the National Stadium, over a railroad bridge, with a very imposing view of the University buildings against the skyline. But everything was so reminiscent of New York in winter that even as I sat at 9:30 P.M. after dinner, writing, looking through the blinds, there was the sound of a train and light on the skyline, and every now and then the tail lights of an auto curving around between the railroad bridge and the hotel. And it felt like a hundred nights that I remembered along Riverside Drive, except that just on the edge of the picture was the golden onion-shaped dome of a Russian Orthodox church.

Before dinner I took a short walk. It was already growing dark, but down the street from the hotel was the Stadium stop on the Metro, which is a subway. I walked down there and into the Metro station and I stood in front of the escalators for awhile just watching the faces of the people coming and going. It felt like instant 14th Street of my childhood, before Blacks and Latins colored New York, except everyone was much more orderly and the whole place seemed much less crowded. The thing that was really strangest of all for the ten minutes that I stood there was that there were no Black people. And the token collector and the station manager were women. The station was very large and very beautiful and very clean — shockingly, strikingly, enjoyably clean. The whole station looked like a theater lobby — bright brass and mosaics and shining chandeliers. Even when they were rushing, and in Moscow there's always a kind of rush, people lack the desperation of New York. One thing that characterized all of these people was a pleasantness in their faces, a willingness to smile, at least at me, a stranger. It was a strange contrast to the grimness of the weather.

There are some Black people around the hotel and I inquired of Helen about the Patrice Lumumba University. This is a university located in Moscow for students from African countries. There were many Africans in and around the hotel when I got back from the Metro station and I think many of them were here for the Conference. Interestingly enough, most of them speak Russian and I don't. When I went downstairs to dinner, I almost quailed in front of the linguistic task because I could not even find out where I was supposed to sit, or whether I should wait to be seated. Whenever the alphabet is unfamiliar, there are absolutely no cues to a foreign language. A young Black man swaggered across my eyesight with that particular swagger of fine, young Black men wanting to be noticed and I said, "Do you speak English?" "Yes," he said and started walking very rapidly away from me. So I walked back to him and when I tried to ask him whether I should sit down or wait to be seated, I realized the poor boy did not understand a word that I said. At that point I pulled out my two trusty phrase books and proceeded to order myself a very delicious dinner of white wine, boiled fish soup that was lemon piquant, olive rich, and fresh mackerel, delicate, grilled sturgeon with pickled sauce, bread, and even a glass of tea. All of this was made possible by great tenacity and daring on my part, and the smiling forebearance of a very helpful waiter who brought out one of the cooks from the kitchen to help with the task of deciphering my desires.

II

It's very cold in Moscow. The day I arrived it snowed in the morning and it snowed again today, and this is September 16th. My guide, Helen, put her finger on it very accurately. She said that life in Moscow is a constant fight against the cold weather, and that living is only a triumph against death by freezing. Maybe because of the cold, or maybe because of the shortage of food in the war years, but everyone eats an enormous amount here. Tonight, because of a slight error on the part of the waitress, Helen had two dinners and thought very little about eating them both. And no one is terribly fat, but I think that has a good deal to do with the weather. We had wine at dinner tonight, and wine seems to be used a lot to loosen up one's tongue. It almost seems a prescription. At every dinner meal there are always three glasses: one for water, one for wine, and one for vodka, which flows like water, and with apparently as little effect upon Russians.

A group from the conference with our Intourist guides went sightseeing today. It's hard to believe that today's Sunday because the whole city seems so full of weekday life, so intent on its own purposes, that it makes the week seem extended by an extra day. We saw the Novagrodsky Convent Museum and the brilliant, saucy golden onion steeples that shock me back from the feeling this is Manhattan. We went to see the University and of course many plaques for many heroes, but I never saw one that moved me as much as the tough old lady coming in on Aeroflot. And the Bolshoi Ballet Theatre. It was rainy and grey and overcast — a New York December day — and very imposing in the way the Grand Concourse at 161st Street in the Bronx can be imposing in the middle of December, or Columbus Circle. The golden onion steeples on some older buildings are beautiful and they glisten all the time, even in this weather, which makes them look like joyful promises on the landscape, or fairy palaces, and the lovely colors of greens, whites, yellows and oranges decorating and outlining windows make a wonderfully colorful accent in the greyness. I hope that I get a chance to see the Pushkin Museum.

I was interviewed by a sweetly astute, motherly woman who was one of the members of the Union of Soviet Writers. She was doing a study of "Negro policy," as she said, and of course she was very interested in women in the States. We talked for a good two hours and one of the things I told her was about the old woman on the plane with the medals, and I asked her if she had any idea what they were. She said the woman was probably an older farm worker who had been awarded and named a

"Hero of the Republic." Those were mostly given to people who worked very hard, she said. It was interesting because earlier, at lunch, I had seen a side of Helen, my interpreter, that surprised me. She was quite out of sorts with one of the waitresses who did not wait on her quickly enough, and it does take a long time to get waited on. Helen made a remark that the workers rule the country, and her manner and response to that seemed to be one of disgust, or at least rather put-off. I think Helen felt that she was being discriminated against, or that she was at a disadvantage, because she was an "intellectual," a translator as well as an interpreter. Which struck me as an odd kind of snobbishness because Helen worked at least as hard, if not harder, than any waitress, running after me and living my life as well as hers. Because always, she stuck to me like white on rice.

We were at the University and our guide was talking to us, in English, about the buildings, which had been built during Stalin's time. Material had been brought down from the Ukraine to sink into the earth to build such buildings because Moscow, unlike New York, is not built upon bedrock. This strikes me as strange, that this city of oversize, imposing stone buildings should not be grounded on bedrock. It's like it remains standing on human will. While we were standing in front of the reflecting pool having this discussion, a little tow-headed boy sidled up to me with a completely international air, all of ten years old, stood in front of me and with a furtive sideways gesture, flipped his hand open. In the center of his little palm was a button-pin of a red star with a soldier in the middle of it. I was completely taken aback because I did not know what the kid wanted and I asked Helen who brushed the child off and shooed him away so quickly I didn't have a chance to stop her. Then she told me that he wanted to trade for American buttons. That little kid had stood off to the side and watched all of these strange Black people, and he had managed to peg me as an American because, of course, Americans are the only ones who go around wearing lots and lots of buttons, and he had wanted to trade his red star button. I was touched by the child, and also because I couldn't help but think that it was Sunday and he was probably hitting all the tourist spots. I'm sure his parents did not know where he was, and I really wondered what his mother would do if she knew.

The woman from the Writers' Union who was doing her book on Negro policy was, I'd say, a little older than I was, probably in her early fifties, and her husband had been killed in the war. She had no children. She offered these facts about herself as soon as we sat down, talking openly about her life, as everybody seemingly does here. I say *seemingly* because it only goes so far. And she, like my guide and most women here, both young and old, seem to mourn the lack of men. At the same time they appear to have shaken off many of the traditional role-playing devices vis-a-vis men. Almost everyone I've met has lost someone in what they call the "Great Patriotic War," which is our Second World War.

I was interviewed by Oleg this evening, one of the officials of the Union of Soviet Writers, the people who had invited me to Russia and who were footing the bill. In my interview with him I learned the hotel that we're staying in was originally a youth hostel and Oleg apologized because it was not as "civilized," so he said, as other Moscow hotels. I came across this term *civilized* before, and I wondered whether it was a term used around Americans or whether it meant up to American standards. Increasingly I get a feeling that American standards are sort of an unspoken norm, and that whether one resists them, or whether one adopts them, they are there to be reckoned with. This is rather disappointing. But coming back to the hotel, I notice that the fixtures here *are* a little shabby, but they *do* work, and the studio beds are a bit adolescent in size, but they are comfortable. For a youth hostel it's better than I would ever hope for. Of course, I can't help but wonder why the African-Asian Conference people should be housed in a youth hostel, particularly an "uncivilized" one, but I don't imagine that I'll ever get an answer to that. All hotel rooms cost the same in the Soviet Union. Utilities, from my conversation with Helen while we were riding the Metro down to send a cable, utilities are very inexpensive. The gas to cook with costs sixteen kopecs a month which is less than one ruble (about $3.00) and the most electricity Helen says that she uses, when she's translating all day long in winter, costs three rubles a month. That is very expensive, she says. The two-room apartment which she and her mother share costs eight rubles a month.

Oleg does not speak English, or does not converse in English. Like many other people I was to meet during my stay in Russia, he understands English although he does not let on. Oleg said through Helen that he wants me to know it was very important for us to meet other writers and that the point of the Conference was for us to get together. I thanked him for the twenty-five rubles I had been given as soon as I arrived here in Moscow, which I have been told was a gift from the Union of Soviet Writers for pocket money. I spoke of the oppressed people all over the world, meeting to touch and to share, I spoke of South Africa and their struggle. Oleg said something very curious. "Yes, South Africa is really very bad. It is like a sore upon the body that will not heal." This sounded to me both removed and proprietary. Unclear. Willy, my South African poet friend, lives in Tanzania now and he may be here, which I am very excited about.

III

We traveled south to Uzbekistan for the Conference, a five-hour journey that became seven because of delays. We arrived in Tashkent after dark following a long, exhausting plane ride. As I have said, Russian planes are incredibly packed, every single inch being taken up in seats. They absolutely utilize their air space. Even coming from New York to Moscow it was like air mass transit. Certainly from Moscow to Tashkent this was true since there were 150 delegates to the African-Asian Writers Conference, myself, one observer, interpreters, and press personnel. All together, a traveling group of about 250 people, which is a large group to move around a country at least four or five times the size of the United States (and in a standard, not wide-bodied, plane).

As we descended the plane in Tashkent, it was deliciously hot and smelled like Accra, Ghana. At least it seemed to me that it did, from the short ride from the airport to the hotel. The road to the city had lots of wood and white marble all around broad avenues, and bright street lights. The whole town of Tashkent had been rebuilt after the 1966 earthquake. We arrived tired and hot, to a welcome that would make your heart grow still, then sing. Can you imagine 250 of us, weary, cramped, hungry, disoriented, overtalked, underfed? It is after dark. We step out of the plane and there before us are over a hundred people and TV cameras, and lights, and two or three hundred little children dressed in costumes with bunches of flowers that they thrust upon each of us as we walked down the ramp from the plane. "Surprise!" Well, you know, it was a surprise. Pure and simple, and I was pretty damn well surprised. I was surprised at the gesture, hokey or not, at the mass participation in it. Most of all, I was surprised at my response to it; I felt genuinely welcomed.

So off to the hotel we went and I had the distinct feeling here, for the first time in Russia, that I was meeting warm-blooded people; in the sense of contact unavoided, desires and emotions possible, the sense that there was something hauntingly, personally familiar — not in the way the town looks because it looked like nothing I'd ever seen before, night and the minarets — but the tempo of life felt hotter, quicker than in Moscow; and in place of Moscow's determined pleasantness, the people displayed a kind of warmth that was very engaging. They are an Asian people in Tashkent. Uzbeki. They look like the descendants of Ghengis Khan, some of whom I'm sure they are. They are Asian and they are Russian. They think and speak and consider themselves Russian, for all intents and purposes so far as I can see, and I really wonder how they manage that. On the other hand, the longer I stayed the more I realized some of the personal tensions between North Russian and Uzbek are national and some racial.

There are only four sisters in this whole conference. In the plane coming to Tashkent, I sat with the three other African women and we exchanged chitchat for 5½ hours about our respective children, about our ex-old men, all very, very heterocetera.

IV

Tashkent is divided into two parts. There's the old part that survived the huge earthquake of 1966, and there's the newer part which is on the outskirts of old Tashkent. It's very new and very modern, rebuilt in a very short time after the earthquake that practically totaled the area. It was rebuilt by labor from all over the Soviet Union. People came from the Ukraine, from Byelo-Russia, from all over, and they rebuilt the city. And there are many different styles of architecture in the new part of town because every group who came built their own type of building. It's almost a memorial to what can be done when a large group of people work together. It was one of the things that impressed me greatly during my stay in Tashkent. The old part, which is really the center of Tashkent, looks very, very much like a town in Ghana or Dahomey, say Kumasi or Cotonou. In the daylight it looks so much like some parts of West Africa that I could scarcely believe it. In fact, if Moscow is New York in another space, in another color — because both New York and Moscow have a little over eight million population and should apparently have many of the same problems, but Moscow seems to have handled them very differently — if Moscow is New York, Tashkent is Accra. It is African in so many ways — the stalls, the mix of the old and the new, the corrugated tin roofs on top of adobe houses. The corn smell in the plaza, although the plazas were more modern than in West Africa. Even some flowers and trees, Calla lilies. But the red laterite smell of the earth was different.

The people here in Tashkent, which is quite close to the Iranian border, are very diverse, and I am impressed by their apparent unity, by the ways in which the Russian and the Asian people seem to be able to function in a multinational atmosphere that requires of them that they get along, whether or not they are each other's favorite people. And it's not that there are no individuals who are nationalists, or racists, but that the taking of a state position against nationalism, against racism is what makes it possible for a society like this to function. And of course the next step in that process must be the personal element. I don't see anyone attempting or even suggesting this phase, however, and that is troublesome, for without this step socialism remains at the mercy of an incomplete vision, imposed from the outside. We have internal desires but outside controls. But at least there is a climate here that seems to encourage those questions. I asked Helen about the Jews, and she was rather evasive, I think, saying only that there were Jews in government. The basic position seems to be one of a presumption of equality, even though there is sometimes a large gap between the expectation and the reality.

We visited a film studio and saw several children's cartoons which handled their themes beautifully, deeply, with great humor, and most notably, without the kind of violence that we have come to associate with cartoons. They were truly delightful.

After two very busy days of meetings in Tashkent, we started out at about 7:30 one morning by bus for Samarkand, the fabulous city of Tamerlane the Great. After a short snooze on the bus I began to feel a little more human, to look about me and the countryside. We're heading southeast from Tashkent, and Tashkent was southeast of Moscow. The countryside is very beautiful. It feels strange and familiar at the same time. This is cotton country. Miles and miles of it, and trainloads of students were coming south from Moscow on a two-week vacation to party and pick cotton. There was a holiday atmosphere all around. We passed through small villages where I could see little markets with women sitting cross-ankled on the bare earth selling a few cabbages or a small tray of fruit. And walls, behind which you could see adobe houses. Even the walls themselves reminded me very much of West Africa, made of a clay mud that cracks in the same old familiar patterns that we saw over and over again in Kumasi and south of Accra. Only here the clay is not red, but a light beige, and that is to remind me that this is the USSR and not Ghana or Dahomey. Of course, the faces are white. There are other differences that creep through also. The towns and the villages are really in very good repair and there is a powerful railroad running parallel to our road. Long, efficient looking trains and tanker cars and ten-car passenger trains pass by us, going through switch houses with blue and white ceramic tiles and painted roofs, all managed by women. Everything looks massive, bigger, in Russia. The roads are wider, the trains longer, the buildings bigger. The ceilings are higher. Everything seems to be on a larger scale.

We stopped for a harvest festival lunch at a collective farm, complete with the prerequisite but very engaging cultural presentation, while vodka flowed. Then we all danced and sang together with the busloads of students who had come to help pick cotton. Later on along the roads there were literally hills of cotton being loaded onto trains.

Each town that we pass through has a cafe, where the villagers can come and spend an evening or chat or talk or watch TV or listen to propaganda, who knows, but where they can meet. And all over, in between very old looking villages, there are also new four story buildings in progress, factories, new apartment houses. Trains full of building slabs and other kinds of materials, coal and rock and tractors pass by, even one with row after row after row of small automobiles. There are three different Russian automobiles. This is the cheapest, and most popular – hundreds and hundreds of cars stacked, all the same lemon color. Obviously, that month the factory was producing yellow.

I watched all of this industry pass and it came through to me on that bus ride down to Samarkand that this land was not industrial so much as it was industrious. There was a flavor of people working hard and doing things and it was very attractive. On top of that, I learned that this area between Tashkent and Samarkand was once known as the "Hungry Desert" because although it was fertile, no rain ever fell and it was covered with a coat of salt. Through technology devised to lift the salt, and a great deal of human hands and engineering, this whole area has been made to bloom, and it really does bloom. It is being farmed, mostly with cotton. People live here and there are massive irrigation ditches and pipes that maintain trees where there are towns and collective farms. All through Uzbekistan the feeling of a desert having been reclaimed and bearing huge fruit is very constant. Later on, as we headed on south after the great feast, we stopped at an oasis, and I picked some desert flowers that were growing — small little scrub flowers that were growing in the sand. And just for so, I tasted one of them and as honeysuckle is sweet, so is this flower salt. It was as if the earth itself was still producing salt or still pouring salt into its products.

There's very beautiful marble throughout Uzbekistan. The stairs of the hotels and sometimes the streets have a beautiful pink and green marble. That was in Tashkent, which means "Stone City." But on this ride from Tashkent to Samarkand I saw no stones or rocks of any kind near the road. I don't know why, except that it is a reclaimed desert. The roads felt very good, and they were very broad because of course there was always heavy machinery and trucking traveling back and forth.

We had another glowing welcome in Gulstan, which means the "Hungry Desert." This is now the village of roses. We visited a collective farm, went into a house, saw the kindergarten. The woman's house into which we went was very impressive, as I said to someone later at lunch who asked me what I thought. I said, "She lives better than I do," and in some ways she did. The collective farm in Gulstan, called the Leningrad Collective, is one of the wealthiest collectives in the area. I will never know the name of the very kind young woman who opened her home to me, but I also will not forget her. She offered me the hospitality of her house, and even though we did not speak the same language, I felt that she was a woman like myself, wishing that all of our children could live in peace upon their own earth, somehow make fruitful the power of their own hands. Through Helen, she spoke about her three children, one of whom was only a nursing infant, and I spoke of my two. I spoke in English and she spoke in Russian, but I felt very strongly that our hearts spoke the same tongue.

I was reminded of her a few days later in Samarkand when Fikre, an Ethiopian student at Patrice Lumumba University, and I went shopping in the market. I remember the Moslem woman who came up to me in the marketplace, and she brought her little boy up to me asking Fikre if I had a little boy also. She said that she had never seen a Black woman before, that she had seen Black men, but she had never seen a Black woman, and that she so much liked the way I looked that she just wanted to bring her little boy and find out if I had a little boy, too. Then we blessed each other and spoke good words and then she passed on.

There was the accomplished and very eloquent young Asian woman, an anthropology student, she said, who acted as our museum guide in Samarkand and shared her great store of historical knowledge with us. The night that we arrived in Samarkand and again the next day in looking through the museums, I felt that there were many things we were not seeing. For instance, we passed a case where there are a number of coins which I recognized as ancient Chinese coins because I'd used them for casting the I Ching. I asked our guide if these were from China. She acted as if I'd said a dirty word. And she said, "No, these were from right here in Samarkand." Now obviously they had been traded, and that was the whole point, but of course I couldn't read the Russian explanation under it, and she evidently took great offense at my use of the word *China*. In all of the women I've met here I feel an air of security and awareness of their own powers as women, as producers, and as human beings that is very affirming. But I also feel a stony rigidity, a resistance to questioning that frightens me, saddens me, because it feels destructive of progress as process.

We arrived in Samarkand about 9:30 P.M., quite wearied by a very full day. We got into the main square just in time to catch the last light-show at Tamerlane's tomb. The less said about that the better. But the following day, Helen, Fikre, and I played hooky from one mausoleum and ran across the street and went to a market. It is very reassuring and good as always. People in markets find a way of getting down to the essentials of I have, you want; you have, I want.

The tile tombs and the midrasas (ancient schools) of Samarkand are truly beautiful, intricate, and still. Incredibly painstaking work is being done to restore them. I could feel stillness in my bones, walking through these places, knowing that so much history had been buried there. I found two feathers in the Tomb of Bebe, Timor's favorite wife, and I felt almost as if I had come there to find them. The Tomb of Bebe has beautiful minarets, but the Tomb itself was never used. The mosque was never used. There is a story that Bebe was Tamerlane's favorite wife and he "loved her with all of his heart." However, he had many, many journeys to go upon and he left her so often that he broke her heart and she died. When he returned and found she was dead, he was very upset because he had loved her so much, and he vowed that he would build the biggest mausoleum in the world, the most ornate mosque for her, and that is what he did. But then, just before it was completed, it collapsed. They say it was due to an error of the architect, but it was never used. One up for the lady shades.

The tile tombs and the midrasas are engrossing, but it's the market that caught my heart. We went later in that afternoon to another meeting of solidarity for the oppressed people of Somewhere. The only thing that I was quite sure of was that it was not for the oppressed Black people of America, which point, of course, I had questioned a number of days before and was still awaiting a reply. So we stood in the hot sun at the porcelain factory and it almost baked my brains, and I thought about a lot of things. The peoples of the Soviet Union, in many respects, impress me as people who can not yet afford to be honest. When they can be they will either blossom into a marvel or sink into decay. What gets me about the United States is that it pretends to be honest and therefore has so little room to move toward hope. I think that in America there are certain kinds of problems and in Russia there are certain kinds of problems, but basically, when you find people who start from a position where human beings are at the core, as opposed to a position where profit is at the core, the solutions can be very different. I wonder how similar human problems will be solved. But I am not always convinced that human beings are at the core here, either, although there is more lip service done to that idea than in the U.S.

I had a meeting the following day with a Madam Izbalkhan, who was the head of the Uzbekistan Society of Friendship. This meeting came about as a result of my request for clarification of my status here at the Conference. When all was said and done, why was there no meeting for oppressed peoples of Black

America? Enough said. Madam Izbalkhan talked two hours and she essentially said, well, here's what our revolution has done for us. And I felt she was implying that any time you want to get yours going, you know, be our guest, just don't expect us to be involved.

But she talked most movingly of the history of the women of Uzbekistan, a history which deserves more writing about than I can give it here. The ways in which the women of this area, from 1924 on, fought to come out from behind complete veiling, from Moslem cloister to the twentieth century. How they gave their lives to go bare-faced, to be able to read. Many of them fought and many of them died very terrible deaths in this battle, killed by their own fathers and brothers. It is a story of genuine female heroism and persistence. I thought of the South African women in 1956 who demonstrated and died rather than carry passbooks. For the Uzbeki women, revolution meant being able to show their faces and go to school, and they died for it. A bronze statue stands in a square of Samarkand, monument to the fallen women and their bravery. Madam went on to discuss the women of modern Uzbekistan and how there was now full equality between the sexes. How many women now headed collective farms, how many women Ministers. She said there were a great many ways in which women governed; there was no difference between men and women now in the Union of Soviet Socialist Republics. I was touched by these statistics, of course, but I also felt that there was a little more to it than met the eye. It sounded too easy, too pat. Madam spoke of the daycare centers, of kindergartens where children could be cared for on collective farms. The kindergartens are free in large cities like Moscow and Tashkent. But in Samarkand, there's a nominal fee of about two rubles a month, which is very little, she said. I asked her one question, whether "men are encouraged to work in the kindergartens to give the children a gentle male figure at an early age." Madam Izbalkhan hesitated for a moment. "No," she said. "We like to believe that when the children come to the kindergarten they acquire a second mother."

Madam Izbalkhan was a very strong and beautiful and forthright woman, excellently in charge of her facts, with a great deal of presence, and I returned from my meeting with her almost overwhelmed and over-graped.

The grapes in Uzbekistan are incredible 'fruit. They seem to have a life of their own. They're called "the bridesmaid's little finger," and that's about the size of them. They're very long, and green, and they're absolutely the most delicious.

I came away with revolutionary women in my head. But I feel very much now still that we, Black Americans, exist alone in the mouth of the dragon. As I've always suspected, outside of rhetoric and proclamations of solidarity, there is no help, except ourselves. When I asked directly about the USSR's *attitude* toward American racism, Madam said reproachfully that of course the USSR cannot interfere in the internal affairs of any other nation. I wish now I had asked her about Russian Jews.

In Samarkand, Helen and I went looking for a fruit market. She inquired directions from a man who had passed by with either his little girl or his granddaughter, but I tend to think his little girl because so many of the adults here in Uzbekistan look much older than they are. It must be a quality of the dry air. Anyway, Helen stopped to inquire directions to the market and this gave him an opening, as frequently happens in Russia, to discuss anything. He wanted to know from Helen whether I was from Africa, and when he heard I was from America, then he really wanted to discuss American Black people. There seems to be quite an interest in Black Americans among the peoples of Russia, but it's an interest that is played down somewhat. Fikre, my Ethiopian companion who studied at the university, was often questioned about me in Russian. I had developed enough of an ear for the language to be able to notice that. Fikre frequently did not say I was from America. Most people in Tashkent and Samarkand who I met thought I was African or from Cuba, and everyone is also very interested in Cuba. This fascination with all things American is something that keeps coming up over and over again.

This man wanted to know from me whether American Black people were allowed to go to school. I said yes, and Helen said yes to him, and then he wanted to know if we were allowed to teach, and I said yes, I was a professor at the University of the

City of New York. And he was surprised at that. He said that he had seen a television program one time about the Black people of America. That we had no jobs. So Helen started to answer him and he stopped her. Then she angrily said he wanted me to speak because he wanted to look at my face so he could see how I answered. I told Helen to tell him that the question was not that we could never go to college, but that frequently even when Black people went to college, we had no jobs when we came out. That it was more difficult for Black people to find work and make any kind of living, and that the percentage of unemployment among American Black people was far higher than that of American white people.

He pondered that a little while and then he asked, do Black people have to pay for their doctors, too? Because that's what TV programs had said. I smiled a little at this and told him it's not only Black people who have to pay for doctors and medical care; all people in America have to. Ah, he said. And suppose you don't have the money to pay? Well, I said, if you don't have the money to pay, sometimes you died. And there was no mistaking my gesture, even though he had to wait for the translator to translate it. We left him looking absolutely nonplussed, standing in the middle of the square with his mouth open and his hand under his chin staring after me, as in utter amazement that human beings could die from lack of medical care. It's things like that that keep me dreaming about Russia long after I've returned.

There's much that I think that Russian people now take for granted. I think they take for granted free hospitalization and medical care. They take for granted free universities and free schooling as well as the presumption of universal bread, even with a rose or two, although no meat. We are all more blind to what we have than to what we have not.

One night after midnight, Fikre and I were walking through a park in Tashkent and we were approached by a Russian man with whom Fikre had a short, sharp conversation, after which the man bowed and walked away. Fikre would not tell me what they'd said, but I had the strong feeling he had tried to pick one of us up, either Fikre or me. Tashkent is, in some respects, a

Russian playground. I asked Fikre what the Soviet position was on homosexuality, and Fikre answered that there was no public position because it wasn't a public matter. Of course, I know better than that, but I have very few inroads into finding out the truth, and Helen is much too proper to discuss anything sexual.

V

The last few days after we returned to Moscow I got to meet one woman I had noticed all through the Conference. She was an Eskimo woman. Her name was Toni and she's Chukwo. They are from the part of Russia closest to Alaska, the part that wasn't sold by the Russians, across the Bering Straits. Toni did not speak English and I didn't speak Russian, but I felt as if we were making love that last night through our interpreters. I still don't know if she knew what was going on or not, but I suspect that she did.

I had been extremely moved by her presentation earlier in the day. We sat down to dinner, about ten of us, and Toni started speaking to me through our interpreters. She said that she had been searching for my eyes in the crowd all through her speech because she felt as if she were talking to my heart. And that when she sang the little song that she did, she sang it for a beginning that she hoped for all of our people. And this lady cast, let me tell you, a very powerful spell. There are only fourteen thousand Chukwo people left. In her speech at one point she said, "It is a very sad thing when a whole people ceases to exist." And then she sang a little song which she said her people sing whenever something new happens. Her dark round eyes and seal-heavy hair flashed and swung in time to her music. It sent a chill down my spine at the time, because although there are 21 million Black Americans, I feel like we're an endangered species too, and how sad for our cultures to die. I felt as if we alone, of all the people at the Conference, shared that knowledge and that threat, Toni and I. At dinner Toni kept telling me how beautiful I was, and how it was not only my beauty that she would carry with her always but my words, and that we should share our joys as well as our sorrows, and someday our children would be able to speak freely with each other. She made toast after toast to women and to their strength. All of this was through our interpreters. I was trying to decide what to make of all this when Toni got up, moved over, and sat down beside me. She touched my knee and kissed me, and so we sat all through dinner. We held hands and we kissed, but any time we spoke to each other, it was done through our interpreters, blond Russian girls who smirked as they translated our words. I suppose Toni and I connected somewhere in the middle of the Aleutians.

She kissed my picture on my book before she got up, thanked us for dinner, and went off with the male Latvian delegate from Riga.

VI

Now it is back to Moscow again, which is still cold and rainy. Moscow across rainy rooftops looks about as dreary as New York does, except the skyline is broken up by huge building cranes. There is an incredible amount of building, it appears, going on all the time in Moscow. There is in New York also, but it's not so obvious on the skyline. The buildings are not built in solid blocks the way they are in New York. You'll have perhaps two large apartment houses to a block, set at different angles, with a lot of greenery and perhaps some parks in between. In other words, it appears that quite a bit of thought has been given to urban planning and how people like or need to move about where they are. Both New York and Moscow have a population of about eight million and in Moscow it is possible and pleasant to walk out after dark without fear. Crime on the streets seems not at all a problem in Moscow. The official reason why and the actual reason why may be very different, but it is a fact. I was struck by the sight of many people, even children, walking through the parks after sundown.

Earlier, when I had first come to Moscow from the airport, I had noticed quite heavy steady traffic, but there did not appear to be a traffic jam or great delay although this was the time when most people were coming home from work. It seemed quite an achievement in a city of eight million people, and I thought Moscow must be handling her problems of urban transportation in a new and creative way. Of course, when I saw the Metro, I realized why. Not only are the stations spotlessly clean, but the trains are quick and comfortable, and I'd never really thought that it could be an actual joy to ride on the subways.

VII

It will take a while and a lot of dreams to metabolize all I've seen and felt in these hectic two weeks. I haven't even discussed the close bonding I felt with some of the African writers and how difficult it was to get to know others. I have no reason to believe Russia is a free society. I have no reason to believe Russia is a classless society. Russia does not even appear to be a strictly egalitarian society. But bread does cost a few kopecs a loaf and everybody I saw seemed to have enough of it. Of course, I did not see Siberia, nor a prison camp, nor a mental hospital. But that fact, in a world where most people — certainly most Black people — are on a breadconcern level, seems to me to be quite a lot. If you conquer the bread problem, that gives you at least a chance to look around at the others.

So, for all of the double messages I received (and there were many — because of the places in which I stayed, because of a kind of both deference and unpleasantness that I received as an American, and because no matter how much is said and done, America still appears to have some kind of magic over many countries), no matter what the shortcomings were, there is enthusiasm about the people that I met in Russia, particularly the people I met in Uzbekhistan. And I recognize some of the contradictions and problems that they have. I am deeply suspicious of the double messages that kept coming and of the fact that when they are finished with you (and by *they*, I mean the government), when they are finished with you, they drop you

and you can fall very far. So what's new? I also am intrigued by
the idea that there are writers who are paid to be writers and
that they survive and they wield considerable power. I am also
very well aware that if what they write is not acceptable, then it
never gets read or it never gets printed. So what's new?

But you do have a country there that has the largest reading
population in the world, that prints books of poetry in editions
of 250,000 copies and those copies sell out in three months.
Everywhere you go, even among those miles of cotton being
harvested in the Uzbekhi sun, people are reading, and no matter what you may say about censorship, they are still reading,
and they're reading an awful lot. Some books are pirated from
the West because Russia does not observe International
Copyright. In Samarkhand, Ernest Gaines' *The Autobiography of
Miss Jane Pittman* was the latest best seller. Now, how many
Russian novels in translation have you read this past year?

Poetry Is Not a Luxury*

THE QUALITY OF LIGHT by which we scrutinize our lives has direct bearing upon the product which we live, and upon the changes which we hope to bring about through those lives. It is within this light that we form those ideas by which we pursue our magic and make it realized. This is poetry as illumination, for it is through poetry that we give name to those ideas which are — until the poem — nameless and formless, about to be birthed, but already felt. That distillation of experience from which true poetry springs births thought as dream births concept, as feeling births idea, as knowledge births (precedes) understanding.

As we learn to bear the intimacy of scrutiny and to flourish within it, as we learn to use the products of that scrutiny for power within our living, those fears which rule our lives and form our silences begin to lose their control over us.

For each of us as women, there is a dark place within, where hidden and growing our true spirit rises, "beautiful/and tough as chestnut/stanchions against (y)our nightmare of weakness/"** and of impotence.

These places of possibility within ourselves are dark because they are ancient and hidden; they have survived and grown strong through that darkness. Within these deep places, each

---

* First published in *Chrysalis: A Magazine of Female Culture*, no. 3 (1977).

** From "Black Mother Woman," first published in *From A Land Where Other People Live* (Broadside Press, Detroit, 1973), and collected in *Chosen Poems: Old and New* (W.W. Norton and Company, New York, 1982) p. 53.

one of us holds an incredible reserve of creativity and power, of unexamined and unrecorded emotion and feeling. The woman's place of power within each of us is neither white nor surface; it is dark, it is ancient, and it is deep.

When we view living in the european mode only as a problem to be solved, we rely solely upon our ideas to make us free, for these were what the white fathers told us were precious.

But as we come more into touch with our own ancient, non-european consciousness of living as a situation to be experienced and interacted with, we learn more and more to cherish our feelings, and to respect those hidden sources of our power from where true knowledge and, therefore, lasting action comes.

At this point in time, I believe that women carry within ourselves the possibility for fusion of these two approaches so necessary for survival, and we come closest to this combination in our poetry. I speak here of poetry as a revelatory distillation of experience, not the sterile word play that, too often, the white fathers distorted the word *poetry* to mean — in order to cover a desperate wish for imagination without insight.

For women, then, poetry is not a luxury. It is a vital necessity of our existence. It forms the quality of the light within which we predicate our hopes and dreams toward survival and change, first made into language, then into idea, then into more tangible action. Poetry is the way we help give name to the nameless so it can be thought. The farthest horizons of our hopes and fears are cobbled by our poems, carved from the rock experiences of our daily lives.

As they become known to and accepted by us, our feelings and the honest exploration of them become sanctuaries and spawning grounds for the most radical and daring of ideas. They become a safe-house for that difference so necessary to change and the conceptualization of any meaningful action. Right now, I could name at least ten ideas I would have found intolerable or incomprehensible and frightening, except as they came after dreams and poems. This is not idle fantasy, but a disciplined attention to the true meaning of "it feels right to me." We can train ourselves to respect our feelings and to transpose them into a language so they can be shared. And where that language does not yet exist, it is our poetry which helps to fashion it. Poetry is not only dream and vision; it is the skeleton architecture of our lives. It lays the foundations for a future of change, a bridge across our fears of what has never been before.

Possibility is neither forever nor instant. It is not easy to sustain belief in its efficacy. We can sometimes work long and hard to establish one beachhead of real resistance to the deaths we are expected to live, only to have that beachhead assaulted or threatened by those canards we have been socialized to fear, or by the withdrawal of those approvals that we have been warned to seek for safety. Women see ourselves diminished or softened by the falsely benign accusations of childishness, of nonuniversality, of changeability, of sensuality. And who asks the question: Am I altering your aura, your ideas, your dreams, or am I merely moving you to temporary and reactive action? And even though the latter is no mean task, it is one that must be seen within the context of a need for true alteration of the very foundations of our lives.

The white fathers told us: I think, therefore I am. The Black mother within each of us — the poet — whispers in our dreams: I feel, therefore I can be free. Poetry coins the language to express and charter this revolutionary demand, the implementation of that freedom.

However, experience has taught us that action in the now is also necessary, always. Our children cannot dream unless they live, they cannot live unless they are nourished, and who else will feed them the real food without which their dreams will be no different from ours? "If you want us to change the world someday, we at least have to live long enough to grow up!" shouts the child.

Sometimes we drug ourselves with dreams of new ideas. The head will save us. The brain alone will set us free. But there are no new ideas still waiting in the wings to save us as women, as human. There are only old and forgotten ones, new combinations, extrapolations and recognitions from within ourselves — along with the renewed courage to try them out. And we must constantly encourage ourselves and each other to attempt the heretical actions that our dreams imply, and so many of our old ideas disparage. In the forefront of our move toward change, there is only poetry to hint at possibility made real. Our poems formulate the implications of ourselves, what we feel within and dare make real (or bring action into accordance with), our fears, our hopes, our most cherished terrors.

For within living structures defined by profit, by linear power, by institutional dehumanization, our feelings were not meant to survive. Kept around as unavoidable adjuncts or pleasant pastimes, feelings were expected to kneel to thought as women were expected to kneel to men. But women have survived. As poets. And there are no new pains. We have felt them all already. We have hidden that fact in the same place where we have hidden our power. They surface in our dreams, and it is our dreams that point the way to freedom. Those dreams are made realizable through our poems that give us the strength and courage to see, to feel, to speak, and to dare.

If what we need to dream, to move our spirits most deeply and directly toward and through promise, is discounted as a luxury, then we give up the core — the fountain — of our power, our womanness; we give up the future of our worlds.

For there are no new ideas. There are only new ways of making them felt — of examining what those ideas feel like being lived on Sunday morning at 7 A.M., after brunch, during wild love, making war, giving birth, mourning our dead — while we suffer the old longings, battle the old warnings and fears of being silent and impotent and alone, while we taste new possibilities and strengths.

The Transformation of Silence into Language and Action*

I HAVE COME to believe over and over again that what is most important to me must be spoken, made verbal and shared, even at the risk of having it bruised or misunderstood. That the speaking profits me, beyond any other effect. I am standing here as a Black lesbian poet, and the meaning of all that waits upon the fact that I am still alive, and might not have been. Less than two months ago I was told by two doctors, one female and one male, that I would have to have breast surgery, and that there was a 60 to 80 percent chance that the tumor was malignant. Between that telling and the actual surgery, there was a three-week period of the agony of an involuntary reorganization of my entire life. The surgery was completed, and the growth was benign.

But within those three weeks, I was forced to look upon myself and my living with a harsh and urgent clarity that has left me still shaken but much stronger. This is a situation faced by many women, by some of you here today. Some of what I experienced during that time has helped elucidate for me much of what I feel concerning the transformation of silence into language and action.

---

* Paper delivered at the Modern Language Association's "Lesbian and Literature Panel," Chicago, Illinois, December 28, 1977. First published in *Sinister Wisdom* 6 (1978) and *The Cancer Journals* (Spinsters, Ink, San Francisco, 1980).

In becoming forcibly and essentially aware of my mortality, and of what I wished and wanted for my life, however short it might be, priorities and omissions became strongly etched in a merciless light, and what I most regretted were my silences. Of what had I *ever* been afraid? To question or to speak as I believed could have meant pain, or death. But we all hurt in so many different ways, all the time, and pain will either change or end. Death, on the other hand, is the final silence. And that might be coming quickly, now, without regard for whether I had ever spoken what needed to be said, or had only betrayed myself into small silences, while I planned someday to speak, or waited for someone else's words. And I began to recognize a source of power within myself that comes from the knowledge that while it is most desirable not to be afraid, learning to put fear into a perspective gave me great strength.

I was going to die, if not sooner then later, whether or not I had ever spoken myself. My silences had not protected me. Your silence will not protect you. But for every real word spoken, for every attempt I had ever made to speak those truths for which I am still seeking, I had made contact with other women while we examined the words to fit a world in which we all believed, bridging our differences. And it was the concern and caring of all those women which gave me strength and enabled me to scrutinize the essentials of my living.

The women who sustained me through that period were Black and white, old and young, lesbian, bisexual, and heterosexual, and we all shared a war against the tyrannies of silence. They all gave me a strength and concern without which I could not have survived intact. Within those weeks of acute fear came the knowledge — within the war we are all waging with the forces of death, subtle and otherwise, conscious or not — I am not only a casualty, I am also a warrior.

What are the words you do not yet have? What do you need to say? What are the tyrannies you swallow day by day and attempt to make your own, until you will sicken and die of them, still in silence? Perhaps for some of you here today, I am the face of one of your fears. Because I am woman, because I am Black, because I am lesbian, because I am myself — a Black woman warrior poet doing my work — come to ask you, are you doing yours?

And of course I am afraid, because the transformation of silence into language and action is an act of self-revelation, and that always seems fraught with danger. But my daughter, when I told her of our topic and my difficulty with it, said, "Tell them about how you're never really a whole person if you remain silent, because there's always that one little piece inside you that wants to be spoken out, and if you keep ignoring it, it gets madder and madder and hotter and hotter, and if you don't speak it out one day it will just up and punch you in the mouth from the inside."

In the cause of silence, each of us draws the face of her own fear — fear of contempt, of censure, or some judgment, or recognition, of challenge, of annihilation. But most of all, I think, we fear the visibility without which we cannot truly live. Within this country where racial difference creates a constant, if unspoken, distortion of vision, Black women have on one hand always been highly visible, and so, on the other hand, have been rendered invisible through the depersonalization of racism. Even within the women's movement, we have had to fight, and still do, for that very visibility which also renders us most vulnerable, our Blackness. For to survive in the mouth of this dragon we call america, we have had to learn this first and most vital lesson — that we were never meant to survive. Not as human beings. And neither were most of you here today, Black or not. And that visibility which makes us most vulnerable is that which also is the source of our greatest strength. Because the machine will try to grind you into dust anyway, whether or not we speak. We can sit in our corners mute forever while our sisters and our selves are wasted, while our children are distorted and destroyed, while our earth is poisoned; we can sit in our safe corners mute as bottles, and we will still be no less afraid.

In my house this year we are celebrating the feast of Kwanza, the African-american festival of harvest which begins the day after Christmas and lasts for seven days. There are seven principles of Kwanza, one for each day. The first principle is Umoja, which means unity, the decision to strive for and maintain unity in self and community. The principle for yesterday, the second day, was Kujichagulia — self-determination — the decision to define ourselves, name ourselves, and speak for ourselves, instead of being defined and spoken for by others. Today is the third day of Kwanza, and the principle for today is Ujima — collective work and responsibility — the decision to build and maintain ourselves and our communities together and to recognize and solve our problems together.

Each of us is here now because in one way or another we share a commitment to language and to the power of language, and to the reclaiming of that language which has been made to work against us. In the transformation of silence into language and action, it is vitally necessary for each one of us to establish or examine her function in that transformation and to recognize her role as vital within that transformation.

For those of us who write, it is necessary to scrutinize not only the truth of what we speak, but the truth of that language by which we speak it. For others, it is to share and spread also those words that are meaningful to us. But primarily for us all, it is necessary to teach by living and speaking those truths which we believe and know beyond understanding. Because in this way alone we can survive, by taking part in a process of life that is creative and continuing, that is growth.

And it is never without fear — of visibility, of the harsh light of scrutiny and perhaps judgment, of pain, of death. But we have lived through all of those already, in silence, except death. And I remind myself all the time now that if I were to have been born mute, or had maintained an oath of silence my whole life long for safety, I would still have suffered, and I would still die. It is very good for establishing perspective.

And where the words of women are crying to be heard, we must each of us recognize our responsibility to seek those words out, to read them and share them and examine them in their pertinence to our lives. That we not hide behind the mockeries of separations that have been imposed upon us and which so often we accept as our own. For instance, "I can't possibly teach Black women's writing — their experience is so different from mine." Yet how many years have you spent teaching Plato and Shakespeare and Proust? Or another, "She's a white woman and what could she possibly have to say to me?" Or, "She's a lesbian, what would my husband say, or my chairman?" Or again, "This woman writes of her sons and I have no children." And all the other endless ways in which we rob ourselves of ourselves and each other.

We can learn to work and speak when we are afraid in the same way we have learned to work and speak when we are tired. For we have been socialized to respect fear more than our own needs for language and definition, and while we wait in silence for that final luxury of fearlessness, the weight of that silence will choke us.

The fact that we are here and that I speak these words is an attempt to break that silence and bridge some of those differences between us, for it is not difference which immobilizes us, but silence. And there are so many silences to be broken.

Scratching the Surface: Some Notes on Barriers to Women and Loving*

Racism: *The belief in the inherent superiority of one race over all others and thereby the right to dominance.*

Sexism: *The belief in the inherent superiority of one sex and thereby the right to dominance.*

Heterosexism: *The belief in the inherent superiority of one pattern of loving and thereby its right to dominance.*

Homophobia: *The fear of feelings of love for members of one's own sex and therefore the hatred of those feelings in others.*

THE ABOVE FORMS of human blindness stem from the same root — an inability to recognize the notion of difference as a dynamic human force, one which is enriching rather than threatening to the defined self, when there are shared goals.

To a large degree, at least verbally, the Black community has moved beyond the "two steps behind her man" concept of sexual relations sometimes mouthed as desirable during the sixties. This was a time when the myth of the Black matriarchy as a social disease was being presented by racist forces to redirect our attentions away from the real sources of Black oppression.

For Black women as well as Black men, it is axiomatic that if we do not define ourselves for ourselves, we will be defined by others — for their use and to our detriment. The development

---

* First published in *The Black Scholar*, vol. 9, no. 7 (1978).

of self-defined Black women, ready to explore and pursue our power and interests within our communities, is a vital component in the war for Black liberation. The image of the Angolan woman with a baby on one arm and a gun in the other is neither romantic nor fanciful. When Black women in this country come together to examine our sources of strength and support, and to recognize our common social, cultural, emotional, and political interests, it is a development which can only contribute to the power of the Black community as a whole. It can certainly never diminish it. For it is through the coming together of self-actualized individuals, female and male, that any real advances can be made. The old sexual power relationships based on a dominant/subordinate model between unequals have not served us as a people, nor as individuals.

Black women who define ourselves and our goals beyond the sphere of a sexual relationship can bring to any endeavor the realized focus of completed and therefore empowered individuals. Black women and Black men who recognize that the development of their particular strengths and interests does not diminish the other do not need to diffuse their energies fighting for control over each other. We can focus our attentions against the real economic, political, and social forces at the heart of this society which are ripping us and our children and our worlds apart.

Increasingly, despite opposition, Black women are coming together to explore and to alter those manifestations of our society which oppress us in different ways from those that oppress Black men. This is no threat to Black men. It is only seen as one by those Black men who choose to embody within themselves those same manifestations of female oppression. For instance, no Black man has ever been forced to bear a child he did not want or could not support. Enforced sterilization and unavailable abortions are tools of oppression against Black women, as is rape. Only to those Black men who are unclear about the pathways of their own definition can the self-actualization and self-protective bonding of Black women be seen as a threatening development.

Today, the red herring of lesbian-baiting is being used in the Black community to obscure the true face of racism/sexism. Black women sharing close ties with each other, politically or emotionally, are not the enemies of Black men. Too frequently, however, some Black men attempt to rule by fear those Black women who are more ally than enemy. These tactics are expressed as threats of emotional rejection: "Their poetry wasn't too bad but I couldn't take all those lezzies." The Black man saying this is code-warning every Black woman present interested in a relationship with a man — and most Black women are — that (1) if she wishes to have her work considered by him she must eschew any other allegiance except to him and (2) any woman who wishes to retain his friendship and/or support had better not be "tainted" by woman-identified interests.

If such threats of labelling, vilification and/or emotional isolation are not enough to bring Black women docilely into camp as followers, or persuade us to avoid each other politically and emotionally, then the rule by terror can be expressed physically, as on the campus of a New York State college in the late 1970s, where Black women sought to come together around women's concerns. Phone calls threatening violence were made to those Black women who dared to explore the possibilities of a feminist connection with non-Black women. Some of these women, intimidated by threats and the withdrawal of Black male approval, did turn against their sisters. When threats did not prevent the attempted coalition of feminists, the resulting campus-wide hysteria left some Black women beaten and raped. Whether the threats by Black men actually led to these assaults, or merely encouraged the climate of hostility within which they could occur, the results upon the women attacked were the same.

War, imprisonment, and "the street" have decimated the ranks of Black males of marriageable age. The fury of many Black heterosexual women against white women who date Black men is rooted in this unequal sexual equation within the Black community, since whatever threatens to widen that equation is deeply and articulately resented. But this is essentially unconstructive resentment because it extends sideways only. It can never result in true progress on the issue because it does not question the vertical lines of power or authority, nor the sexist assumptions which dictate the terms of that competition. And the racism of white women might be better addressed where it is less complicated by their own sexual oppression. In this situation it is not the non-Black woman who calls the tune, but rather the Black man who turns away from himself in his sisters or who, through a fear borrowed from white men, reads her strength not as a resource but as a challenge.

All too often the message comes loud and clear to Black women from Black men: "I am the only prize worth having and there are not too many of me, and remember, I can always go elsewhere. So if you want me, you'd better stay in your place which is away from one another, or I will call you 'lesbian' and wipe you out." Black women are programmed to define ourselves within this male attention and to compete with each other for it rather than to recognize and move upon our common interests.

The tactic of encouraging horizontal hostility to becloud more pressing issues of oppression is by no means new, nor limited to relations between women. The same tactic is used to encourage separation between Black women and Black men. In discussions around the hiring and firing of Black faculty at universities, the charge is frequently heard that Black women are more easily hired than are Black men. For this reason, Black women's problems of promotion and tenure are not to be considered important since they are only "taking jobs away from Black men." Here again, energy is being wasted on fighting each other over the pitifully few crumbs allowed us rather than being used, in a joining of forces, to fight for a more realistic ratio of Black faculty. The latter would be a vertical battle against racist policies of the academic structure itself, one which could result in real power and change. It is the structure at the top which desires changelessness and which profits from these apparently endless kitchen wars.

Instead of keeping our attentions focused upon our real needs, enormous energy is being wasted in the Black community today in antilesbian hysteria. Yet women-identified women — those who sought their own destinies and attempted to execute them in the absence of male support — have been around in all of our communities for a long time. As Yvonne Flowers of York College pointed out in a recent discussion, the unmarried aunt, childless or otherwise, whose home and resources were often a welcome haven for different members of the family, was a familiar figure in many of our childhoods. And within the homes of our Black communities today, it is not the Black lesbian who is battering and raping our underage girl-children out of displaced and sickening frustration.

The Black lesbian has come under increasing attack from both Black men and heterosexual Black women. In the same way that the existence of the self-defined Black woman is no threat to the self-defined Black man, the Black lesbian is an emotional threat only to those Black women whose feelings of kinship and love for other Black women are problematic in some way. For so long, we have been encouraged to view each other with suspicion, as eternal competitors, or as the visible face of our own self-rejection.

Yet traditionally, Black women have always bonded together in support of each other, however uneasily and in the face of whatever other allegiances which militated against that bonding. We have banded together with each other for wisdom and strength and support, even when it was only in relationship to one man. We need only look at the close, although highly complex and involved, relationships between African co-wives, or at the Amazon warriors of ancient Dahomey who fought together as the King's main and most ferocious bodyguard. We need only look at the more promising power wielded by the West African Market Women Associations of today, and those governments which have risen and fallen at their pleasure.

In a retelling of her life, a ninety-two-year-old Efik-Ibibio woman of Nigeria recalls her love for another woman:

> I had a woman friend to whom I revealed my secrets. She was very fond of keeping secrets to herself. We acted as husband and wife. We always moved hand in glove and my husband and hers knew about our relationship. The villagers nicknamed us twin

sisters. When I was out of gear with my husband, she would be the one to restore peace. I often sent my children to go and work for her in return for her kindnesses to me. My husband being more fortunate to get more pieces of land than her husband, allowed some to her, even though she was not my co-wife.*

On the West Coast of Africa, the Fon of Dahomey still have twelve different kinds of marriage. One of them is known as "giving the goat to the buck," where a woman of independent means marries another woman who then may or may not bear children, all of whom will belong to the blood line of the first woman. Some marriages of this kind are arranged to provide heirs for women of means who wish to remain "free," and some are lesbian relationships. Marriages like these occur throughout Africa, in several different places among different peoples.** Routinely, the women involved are accepted members of their communities, evaluated not by their sexuality but by their respective places within the community.

While a piece of each Black woman remembers the old ways of another place — when we enjoyed each other in a sisterhood of work and play and power — other pieces of us, less functional, eye one another with suspicion. In the interests of separation, Black women have been taught to view each other as always suspect, heartless competitors for the scarce male, the all-important prize that could legitimize our existence. This dehumanizing denial of self is no less lethal than the dehumanization of racism to which it is so closely allied.

If the recent attack upon lesbians in the Black community is based solely upon an aversion to the idea of sexual contact between members of the same sex (a contact which has existed for ages in most of the female compounds across the African continent), why then is the idea of sexual contact between Black men so much more easily accepted, or unremarked? Is the imagined threat simply the existence of a self-motivated, self-defined Black woman who will not fear nor suffer terrible retribution from the

---

* Iris Andreski, *Old Wives Tales: Life-Stories of African Women* (Schocken Books, New York, 1970), p. 131.

** Melville Herskovits, *Dahomey*, 2 vols. (Northwestern University Press, Evanston, Illinois, 1967), 1:320-322.

gods because she does not necessarily seek her face in a man's eyes, even if he has fathered her children? Female-headed households in the Black community are not always situations by default.

The distortion of relationship which says "I disagree with you, so I must destroy you" leaves us as Black people with basically uncreative victories, defeated in any common struggle. This jugular vein psychology is based on the fallacy that your assertion or affirmation of self is an attack upon my self — or that my defining myself will somehow prevent or retard your self-definition. The supposition that one sex needs the other's acquiescence in order to exist prevents both from moving together as self-defined persons toward a common goal.

This kind of action is a prevalent error among oppressed peoples. It is based upon the false notion that there is only a limited and particular amount of freedom that must be divided up between us, with the largest and juiciest pieces of liberty going as spoils to the victor or the stronger. So instead of joining together to fight for more, we quarrel between ourselves for a larger slice of the one pie. Black women fight between ourselves over men, instead of pursuing and using who we are and our strengths for lasting change; Black women and men fight between ourselves over who has more of a right to freedom, instead of seeing each other's struggles as part of our own and vital to our common goals; Black and white women fight between ourselves over who is the more oppressed, instead of seeing those areas in which our causes are the same. (Of course, this last separation is worsened by the intransigent racism that white women too often fail to, or cannot, address in themselves.)

At a recent Black literary conference, a heterosexual Black woman stated that to endorse lesbianism was to endorse the death of our race. This position reflects acute fright or a faulty reasoning, for once again it ascribes false power to difference. To the racist, Black people are so powerful that the presence of one can contaminate a whole lineage; to the heterosexist, lesbians are so powerful that the presence of one can contaminate the whole sex. This position supposes that if we do not eradicate lesbianism in the Black community, all Black women will become lesbians. It also supposes that lesbians do not have children. Both suppositions are patently false.

As Black women, we must deal with all the realities of our lives which place us at risk as Black women — homosexual or heterosexual. In 1977 in Detroit, a young Black actress, Patricia Cowan, was invited to audition for a play called *Hammer* and was then hammered to death by the young Black male playwright. Patricia Cowan was not killed because she was Black. She was killed because she was a Black woman, and her cause belongs to us all. History does not record whether or not she was a lesbian, but only that she had a four-year-old child.

Of the four groups, Black and white women, Black and white men, Black women have the lowest average wage. This is a vital concern for us all, no matter with whom we sleep.

As Black women we have the right and responsibility to define ourselves and to seek our allies in common cause: with Black men against racism, and with each other and white women against sexism. But most of all, as Black women we have the right and responsibility to recognize each other without fear and to love where we choose. Both lesbian and heterosexual Black women today share a history of bonding and strength to which our sexual identities and our other differences must not blind us.

Uses of the Erotic:
The Erotic as Power*

THERE ARE MANY kinds of power, used and unused, acknowledged or otherwise. The erotic is a resource within each of us that lies in a deeply female and spiritual plane, firmly rooted in the power of our unexpressed or unrecognized feeling. In order to perpetuate itself, every oppression must corrupt or distort those various sources of power within the culture of the oppressed that can provide energy for change. For women, this has meant a suppression of the erotic as a considered source of power and information within our lives.

We have been taught to suspect this resource, vilified, abused, and devalued within western society. On the one hand, the superficially erotic has been encouraged as a sign of female inferiority; on the other hand, women have been made to suffer and to feel both contemptible and suspect by virtue of its existence.

It is a short step from there to the false belief that only by the suppression of the erotic within our lives and consciousness can women be truly strong. But that strength is illusory, for it is fashioned within the context of male models of power.

As women, we have come to distrust that power which rises from our deepest and nonrational knowledge. We have been warned against it all our lives by the male world, which values

* Paper delivered at the Fourth Berkshire Conference on the History of Women, Mount Holyoke College, August 25, 1978. First published as a pamphlet by Out & Out Books. Now published as a pamphlet by Kore Press.

this depth of feeling enough to keep women around in order to exercise it in the service of men, but which fears this same depth too much to examine the possibilities of it within themselves. So women are maintained at a distant/inferior position to be psychically milked, much the same way ants maintain colonies of aphids to provide a life-giving substance for their masters.

But the erotic offers a well of replenishing and provocative force to the woman who does not fear its revelation, nor succumb to the belief that sensation is enough.

The erotic has often been misnamed by men and used against women. It has been made into the confused, the trivial, the psychotic, the plasticized sensation. For this reason, we have often turned away from the exploration and consideration of the erotic as a source of power and information, confusing it with its opposite, the pornographic. But pornography is a direct denial of the power of the erotic, for it represents the suppression of true feeling. Pornography emphasizes sensation without feeling.

The erotic is a measure between the beginnings of our sense of self and the chaos of our strongest feelings. It is an internal sense of satisfaction to which, once we have experienced it, we know we can aspire. For having experienced the fullness of this depth of feeling and recognizing its power, in honor and self-respect we can require no less of ourselves.

It is never easy to demand the most from ourselves, from our lives, from our work. To encourage excellence is to go beyond the encouraged mediocrity of our society is to encourage excellence. But giving in to the fear of feeling and working to capacity is a luxury only the unintentional can afford, and the unintentional are those who do not wish to guide their own destinies.

This internal requirement toward excellence which we learn from the erotic must not be misconstrued as demanding the impossible from ourselves nor from others. Such a demand incapacitates everyone in the process. For the erotic is not a question only of what we do; it is a question of how acutely and fully we can feel in the doing. Once we know the extent to which we are capable of feeling that sense of satisfaction and completion, we can then observe which of our various life endeavors bring us closest to that fullness.

The aim of each thing which we do is to make our lives and the lives of our children richer and more possible. Within the celebration of the erotic in all our endeavors, my work becomes a conscious decision — a longed-for bed which I enter gratefully and from which I rise up empowered.

Of course, women so empowered are dangerous. So we are taught to separate the erotic demand from most vital areas of our lives other than sex. And the lack of concern for the erotic root and satisfactions of our work is felt in our disaffection from so much of what we do. For instance, how often do we truly love our work even at its most difficult?

The principal horror of any system which defines the good in terms of profit rather than in terms of human need, or which defines human need to the exclusion of the psychic and emotional components of that need — the principal horror of such a system is that it robs our work of its erotic value, its erotic power and life appeal and fulfillment. Such a system reduces work to a travesty of necessities, a duty by which we earn bread or oblivion for ourselves and those we love. But this is tantamount to blinding a painter and then telling her to improve her work, and to enjoy the act of painting. It is not only next to impossible, it is also profoundly cruel.

As women, we need to examine the ways in which our world can be truly different. I am speaking here of the necessity for reassessing the quality of all the aspects of our lives and of our work, and of how we move toward and through them.

The very word *erotic* comes from the Greek word *eros*, the personification of love in all its aspects — born of Chaos, and personifying creative power and harmony. When I speak of the erotic, then, I speak of it as an assertion of the lifeforce of women; of that creative energy empowered, the knowledge and use of which we are now reclaiming in our language, our history, our dancing, our loving, our work, our lives.

There are frequent attempts to equate pornography and eroticism, two diametrically opposed uses of the sexual. Because of these attempts, it has become fashionable to separate the spiritual (psychic and emotional) from the political, to see them as contradictory or antithetical. "What do you mean, a poetic revolutionary, a meditating gunrunner?" In the same way, we have attempted to separate the spiritual and the erotic, thereby reducing the spiritual to a world of flattened affect, a world of the ascetic who aspires to feel nothing. But nothing is farther from the truth. For the ascetic position is one of the highest fear, the gravest immobility. The severe abstinence of the ascetic becomes the ruling obsession. And it is one not of self-discipline but of self-abnegation.

The dichotomy between the spiritual and the political is also false, resulting from an incomplete attention to our erotic knowledge. For the bridge which connects them is formed by the erotic – the sensual – those physical, emotional, and psychic expressions of what is deepest and strongest and richest within each of us, being shared: the passions of love, in its deepest meanings.

Beyond the superficial, the considered phrase, "It feels right to me," acknowledges the strength of the erotic into a true knowledge, for what that means is the first and most powerful guiding light toward any understanding. And understanding is a handmaiden which can only wait upon, or clarify, that knowledge, deeply born. The erotic is the nurturer or nursemaid of all our deepest knowledge.

The erotic functions for me in several ways, and the first is in providing the power which comes from sharing deeply any pursuit with another person. The sharing of joy, whether physical, emotional, psychic, or intellectual, forms a bridge between the sharers which can be the basis for understanding much of what is not shared between them, and lessens the threat of their difference.

Another important way in which the erotic connection functions is the open and fearless underlining of my capacity for joy. In the way my body stretches to music and opens into response, hearkening to its deepest rhythms, so every level upon which I sense also opens to the erotically satisfying experience, whether it is dancing, building a bookcase, writing a poem, examining an idea.

That self-connection shared is a measure of the joy which I know myself to be capable of feeling, a reminder of my capacity for feeling. And that deep and irreplaceable knowledge of my capacity for joy comes to demand from all of my life that it be lived within the knowledge that such satisfaction is possible, and does not have to be called *marriage*, nor *god*, nor *an afterlife*.

This is one reason why the erotic is so feared, and so often relegated to the bedroom alone, when it is recognized at all. For once we begin to feel deeply all the aspects of our lives, we begin to demand from ourselves and from our life-pursuits that they feel in accordance with that joy which we know ourselves to be capable of. Our erotic knowledge empowers us, becomes a lens through which we scrutinize all aspects of our existence, forcing us to evaluate those aspects honestly in terms of their relative meaning within our lives. And this is a grave responsibility, projected from within each of us, not to settle for the convenient, the shoddy, the conventionally expected, nor the merely safe.

During World War II, we bought sealed plastic packets of white, uncolored margarine, with a tiny, intense pellet of yellow coloring perched like a topaz just inside the clear skin of the bag. We would leave the margarine out for a while to soften, and then we would pinch the little pellet to break it inside the bag, releasing the rich yellowness into the soft pale mass of margarine. Then taking it carefully between our fingers, we would knead it gently back and forth, over and over, until the color had spread throughout the whole pound bag of margarine, thoroughly coloring it.

I find the erotic such a kernel within myself. When released from its intense and constrained pellet, it flows through and colors my life with a kind of energy that heightens and sensitizes and strengthens all my experience.

We have been raised to fear the *yes* within ourselves, our deepest cravings. But, once recognized, those which do not enhance our future lose their power and can be altered. The fear of our desires keeps them suspect and indiscriminately powerful, for to suppress any truth is to give it strength beyond endurance. The fear that we cannot grow beyond whatever distortions we may find within ourselves keeps us docile and loyal and obedient, externally defined, and leads us to accept many facets of our oppression as women.

When we live outside ourselves, and by that I mean on external directives only rather than from our internal knowledge and needs, when we live away from those erotic guides from within ourselves, then our lives are limited by external and alien forms, and we conform to the needs of a structure that is not based on human need, let alone an individual's. But when we begin to live from within outward, in touch with the power of the erotic within ourselves, and allowing that power to inform and illuminate our actions upon the world around us, then we begin to be responsible to ourselves in the deepest sense. For as we begin to recognize our deepest feelings, we begin to give up, of necessity, being satisfied with suffering and self-negation, and with the numbness which so often seems like their only alternative in our society. Our acts against oppression become integral with self, motivated and empowered from within.

In touch with the erotic, I become less willing to accept powerlessness, or those other supplied states of being which are not native to me, such as resignation, despair, self-effacement, depression, self-denial.

And yes, there is a hierarchy. There is a difference between painting a back fence and writing a poem, but only one of quantity. And there is, for me, no difference between writing a good poem and moving into sunlight against the body of a woman I love.

This brings me to the last consideration of the erotic. To share the power of each other's feelings is different from using another's feelings as we would use a kleenex. When we look the other way from our experience, erotic or otherwise, we use rather than share the feelings of those others who participate in the experience with us. And use without consent of the used is abuse.

In order to be utilized, our erotic feelings must be recognized. The need for sharing deep feeling is a human need. But within the european-american tradition, this need is satisfied by certain proscribed erotic comings-together. These occasions are almost always characterized by a simultaneous looking away, a pretense of calling them something else, whether a religion, a fit, mob violence, or even playing doctor. And this misnaming of the need and the deed give rise to that distortion which results in pornography and obscenity — the abuse of feeling.

When we look away from the importance of the erotic in the development and sustenance of our power, or when we look away from ourselves as we satisfy our erotic needs in concert with others, we use each other as objects of satisfaction rather than share our joy in the satisfying, rather than make connection with our similarities and our differences. To refuse to be conscious of what we are feeling at any time, however comfortable that might seem, is to deny a large part of the experience, and to allow ourselves to be reduced to the pornographic, the abused, and the absurd.

The erotic cannot be felt secondhand. As a Black lesbian feminist, I have a particular feeling, knowledge, and understanding for those sisters with whom I have danced hard, played, or even fought. This deep participation has often been the forerunner for joint concerted actions not possible before.

But this erotic charge is not easily shared by women who continue to operate under an exclusively european-american male tradition. I know it was not available to me when I was trying to adapt my consciousness to this mode of living and sensation.

Only now, I find more and more women-identified women brave enough to risk sharing the erotic's electrical charge without having to look away, and without distorting the enormously powerful and creative nature of that exchange. Recognizing the power of the erotic within our lives can give us the energy to pursue genuine change within our world, rather than merely settling for a shift of characters in the same weary drama.

For not only do we touch our most profoundly creative source, but we do that which is female and self-affirming in the face of a racist, patriarchal, and anti-erotic society.

Sexism: An American Disease in Blackface*

BLACK FEMINISM is not white feminism in blackface. Black women have particular and legitimate issues which affect our lives as Black women, and addressing those issues does not make us any less Black. To attempt to open dialogue between Black women and Black men by attacking Black feminists seems shortsighted and self-defeating. Yet this is what Robert Staples, Black sociologist, has done in *The Black Scholar*.

Despite our recent economic gains, Black women are still the lowest paid group in the nation by sex and race. This gives some idea of the inequity from which we started. In Staples' own words, Black women in 1979 only "*threaten* to overtake black men" [italics mine] by the "next century" in education, occupation, and income. In other words, the inequity is self-evident; but how is it justifiable?

Black feminists speak as women because we are women and do not need others to speak for us. It is for Black men to speak up and tell us why and how their manhood is so threatened that Black women should be the prime targets of their justifiable rage. What correct analysis of this capitalist dragon within which we live can legitimize the rape of Black women by Black men?

At least Black feminists and other Black women have begun this much-needed dialogue, however bitter our words. At least

* First published as "The Great American Disease" in *The Black Scholar*, vol. 10, no. 9 (May-June 1979) in response to "The Myth of Black Macho: A Response to Angry Black Feminists" by Robert Staples in *The Black Scholar*, vol. 10, no. 8 (March-April 1979).

we are not mowing down our brothers in the street, or bludgeoning them to death with hammers. Yet. We recognize the fallacies of separatist solutions.

Staples pleads his cause by saying capitalism has left the Black man only his penis for fulfillment, and a "curious rage." Is this rage any more legitimate than the rage of Black women? And why are Black women supposed to absorb that male rage in silence? Why isn't that male rage turned upon those forces which limit his fulfillment, namely capitalism? Staples sees in Ntozake Shange's play *For Colored Girls* "a collective appetite for black male blood." Yet it is my female children and my Black sisters who lie bleeding all around me, victims of the appetites of our brothers.

Into what theoretical analysis would Staples fit Patricia Cowan? She answered an ad in Detroit for a Black actress to audition in a play called *Hammer*. As she acted out an argument scene, watched by the playwright's brother and her four-year-old son, the Black male playwright picked up a sledgehammer and bludgeoned her to death. Will Staples' "compassion for misguided black men" bring this young mother back, or make her senseless death more acceptable?

Black men's feelings of cancellation, their grievances, and their fear of vulnerability must be talked about, but not by Black women when it is at the expense of our own "curious rage."

If this society ascribes roles to Black men which they are not allowed to fulfill, is it Black women who must bend and alter our lives to compensate, or is it society that needs changing? And why should Black men accept these roles as correct ones, or anything other than a narcotic promise encouraging acceptance of other facets of their own oppression?

One tool of the Great-American-Double-Think is to blame the victim for victimization: Black people are said to invite lynching by not knowing our place; Black women are said to invite rape and murder and abuse by not being submissive enough, or by being too seductive, or too . . .

Staples' "fact" that Black women get their sense of fulfillment from having children is only a fact when stated out of the mouths of Black men, and any Black person in this country, even a "happily married" woman who has "no pent-up frustrations that need release" (!) is either a fool or insane. This smacks of the oldest sexist canard of all time, that all a woman needs to "keep her quiet" is a "good man." File that one alongside "Some of my best friends are . . ."

Instead of beginning the much-needed dialogue between Black men and Black women, Staples retreats to a defensive stance reminiscent of white liberals of the 60s, many of whom saw any statement of Black pride and self-assertion as an automatic threat to their own identity and an attempt to wipe them out. Here we have an intelligent Black man believing — or at least saying — that any call to Black women to love ourselves (and no one said *only*) is a denial of, or threat to, his Black male identity!

In this country, Black women traditionally have had compassion for everybody else except ourselves. We have cared for whites because we had to for pay or survival; we have cared for our children and our fathers and our brothers and our lovers. History and popular culture, as well as our personal lives, are full of tales of Black women who had "compassion for misguided black men." Our scarred, broken, battered and dead daughters and sisters are a mute testament to that reality. We need to learn to have care and compassion for ourselves, also.

In the light of what Black women often willingly sacrifice for our children and our men, this is a much needed exhortation, no matter what illegitimate use the white media makes of it. This call for self-value and self-love is quite different from narcissism, as Staples must certainly realize. Narcissism comes not out of self-love but out of self-hatred.

The lack of a reasonable and articulate Black male viewpoint on these questions is not the responsibility of Black women. We have too often been expected to be all things to all people and speak everyone else's position but our very own. Black men are not so passive that they must have Black women speak for them. Even my fourteen-year-old son knows that. Black men themselves must examine and articulate their own desires and positions and stand by the conclusions thereof. No point is served by a Black male professional who merely whines at the absence of his viewpoint in Black women's work. Oppressors always expect the oppressed to extend to them the understanding so lacking in themselves.

For Staples to suggest, for instance, that Black men leave their families as a form of male protest against female decision making in the home is in direct contradiction to his own observations in "The Myth of the Black Matriarchy."*

Now I am sure there are still some Black men who marry white women because they feel a white woman can better fit the model of "femininity" set forth in this country. But for Staples to justify that act using the reason it occurs, and take Black women to task for it, is not only another error in reasoning; it is like justifying the actions of a lemming who follows its companions over the cliff to sure death. Because it happens does not mean it should happen, nor that it is functional for the well-being of the individual nor the group.

It is not the destiny of Black america to repeat white america's mistakes. But we will, if we mistake the trappings of success in a sick society for the signs of a meaningful life. If Black men continue to define "femininity" instead of their own desires, and to do it in archaic european terms, they restrict our access to each other's energies. Freedom and future for Blacks does not mean absorbing the dominant white male disease of sexism.

As Black women and men, we cannot hope to begin dialogue by denying the oppressive nature of male privilege. And if Black males choose to assume that privilege for whatever reason — raping, brutalizing, and killing Black women — then ignoring these acts of Black male oppression within our communities can only serve our destroyers. One oppression does not justify another.

It has been said that Black men cannot be denied their personal choice of the woman who meets their need to dominate. In that case, Black women also cannot be denied our personal choices, and those choices are becomingly increasingly self-assertive and female-oriented.

* "The Myth of the Black Matriarchy" by Robert Staples in *The Black Scholar*, vol. 1, no. 3-4 (January-February 1970).

As a people, we most certainly must work together. It would be shortsighted to believe that Black men alone are to blame for the above situations in a society dominated by white male privilege. But the Black male consciousness must be raised to the realization that sexism and woman-hating are critically dysfunctional to his liberation as a Black man because they arise out of the same constellation that engenders racism and homophobia. Until that consciousness is developed, Black men will view sexism and the destruction of Black women as tangential to Black liberation rather than as central to that struggle. So long as this occurs, we will never be able to embark upon that dialogue between Black women and Black men that is so essential to our survival as a people. This continued blindness between us can only serve the oppressive system within which we live.

Men avoid women's observations by accusing us of being too "visceral." But no amount of understanding the roots of Black woman-hating will bring back Patricia Cowan, nor mute her family's loss. Pain is very visceral, particularly to the people who are hurting. As the poet Mary McAnally said, "Pain teaches us to take our fingers OUT the fucking fire."*

If the problems of Black women are only derivatives of a larger contradiction between capital and labor, then so is racism, and both must be fought by all of us. The capitalist structure is a many-headed monster. I might add here that in no socialist country that I have visited have I found an absence of racism or of sexism, so the eradication of both of these diseases seems to involve more than the abolition of capitalism as an institution.

No reasonable Black man can possibly condone the rape and slaughter of Black women by Black men as a fitting response to capitalist oppression. And destruction of Black women by Black men clearly cuts across all class lines.

Whatever the "structural underpinnings" (Staples) for sexism in the Black community may be, it is obviously Black women who are bearing the brunt of that sexism, and so it is in our best interest to abolish it. We invite our Black brothers to join us,

---

* From *We Will Make A River*, poems by Mary McAnnally (West End Press, Cambridge, Massachusetts, 1979), p. 27.

since ultimately that abolition is in their best interests also. For Black men are also diminished by a sexism which robs them of meaningful connections to Black women and our struggles. Since it is Black women who are being abused, however, and since it is our female blood that is being shed, it is for Black women to decide whether or not sexism in the Black community is pathological. And we do not approach that discussion theoretically. Those "creative relationships" which Staples speaks about within the Black community are almost invariably those which operate to the benefit of Black males, given the Black male/female ratio and the implied power balance within a supply and demand situation. Polygamy is seen as "creative," but a lesbian relationship is not. This is much the same as how the "creative relationships" between master and slave were always those benefiting the master.

The results of woman-hating in the Black community are tragedies which diminish all Black people. These acts must be seen in the context of a systematic devaluation of Black women within this society. It is within this context that we become approved and acceptable targets for Black male rage, so acceptable that even a Black male social scientist condones and excuses this depersonalizing abuse.

This abuse is no longer acceptable to Black women in the name of solidarity, nor of Black liberation. Any dialogue between Black women and Black men must begin there, no matter where it ends.

An Open Letter
to Mary Daly

The following letter was written to Mary Daly, author of
Gyn/Ecology,* on May 6, 1979. Four months later, having received no reply, I open it to the community of women.

DEAR MARY,

With a moment of space in this wild and bloody spring,** I
want to speak the words I have had in mind for you. I had
hoped that our paths might cross and we could sit down
together and talk, but this has not happened.

I wish you strength and satisfaction in your eventual victory
over the repressive forces of the University in Boston. I am glad
so many women attended the speak-out, and hope that this
show of joined power will make more space for you to grow and
be within.

Thank you for having *Gyn/Ecology* sent to me. So much of it
is full of import, useful, generative, and provoking. As in *Beyond
God The Father*, many of your analyses are strengthening and
helpful to me. Therefore, it is because of what you have given to
me in the past work that I write this letter to you now, hoping
to share with you the benefits of my insights as you have shared
the benefits of yours with me.

This letter has been delayed because of my grave reluctance to
reach out to you, for what I want us to chew upon here is
neither easy nor simple. The history of white women who are
unable to hear Black women's words, or to maintain dialogue
with us, is long and discouraging. But for me to assume that you
will not hear me represents not only history, perhaps, but an

---

* *Gyn/Ecology: The Metaethics of Radical Feminism* (Beacon Press, Boston, 1978).

** In the spring of 1979, twelve Black women were murdered in the Boston area.

old pattern of relating, sometimes protective and sometimes dysfunctional, which we, as women shaping our future, are in the process of shattering and passing beyond, I hope.

I believe in your good faith toward all women, in your vision of a future within which we can all flourish, and in your commitment to the hard and often painful work necessary to effect change. In this spirit I invite you to a joint clarification of some of the differences which lie between us as a Black and a white woman.

When I started reading *Gyn/Ecology*, I was truly excited by the vision behind your words and nodded my head as you spoke in your First Passage of myth and mystification. Your words on the nature and function of the Goddess, as well as the ways in which her face has been obscured, agreed with what I myself have discovered in my searches through African myth/legend/religion for the true nature of old female power.

So I wondered, why doesn't Mary deal with Afrekete as an example? Why are her goddess images only white, western european, judeo-christian? Where was Afrekete, Yemanje, Oyo, and Mawulisa? Where were the warrior goddesses of the Vodun, the Dahomeian Amazons and the warrior-women of Dan? Well, I thought, Mary has made a conscious decision to narrow her scope and to deal only with the ecology of western european women.

Then I came to the first three chapters of your Second Passage, and it was obvious that you were dealing with noneuropean women, but only as victims and preyers-upon each other. I began to feel my history and my mythic background distorted by the absence of any images of my foremothers in power. Your inclusion of African genital mutilation was an important and necessary piece in any consideration of female ecology, and too little has been written about it. To imply, however, that all women suffer the same oppression simply because we are women is to lose sight of the many varied tools of patriarchy. It is to ignore how those tools are used by women without awareness against each other.

To dismiss our Black foremothers may well be to dismiss where european women learned to love. As an African-american woman in white patriarchy, I am used to having my archetypal experience distorted and trivialized, but it is terribly painful to feel it being done by a woman whose knowledge so much touches my own.

When I speak of knowledge, as you know, I am speaking of that dark and true depth which understanding serves, waits upon, and makes accessible through language to ourselves and others. It is this depth within each of us that nurtures vision.

What you excluded from *Gyn/Ecology* dismissed my heritage and the heritage of all other noneuropean women, and denied the real connections that exist between all of us.

It is obvious that you have done a tremendous amount of work for this book. But simply because so little material on nonwhite female power and symbol exists in white women's words from a radical feminist perspective, to exclude this aspect of connection from even comment in your work is to deny the fountain of noneuropean female strength and power that nurtures each of our visions. It is to make a point by choice.

Then, to realize that the only quotations from Black women's words were the ones you used to introduce your chapter on African genital mutilation made me question why you needed to use them at all. For my part, I felt that you had in fact misused my words, utilized them only to testify against myself as a woman of Color. For my words which you used were no more, nor less, illustrative of this chapter than "Poetry Is Not a Luxury" or any number of my other poems might have been of many other parts of *Gyn/Ecology*.

So the question arises in my mind, Mary, do you ever really read the work of Black women? Did you ever read my words, or did you merely finger through them for quotations which you thought might valuably support an already conceived idea concerning some old and distorted connection between us? This is not a rhetorical question.

To me, this feels like another instance of the knowledge, crone-ology and work of women of Color being ghettoized by a white woman dealing only out of a patriarchal western european frame of reference. Even your words on page 49 of *Gyn/Ecology*, "The strength which Self-centering women find, in finding our Background, is our *own* strength, which we give back to our Selves," have a different ring as we remember the old traditions of power and strength and nurturance found in the female bonding of African women. It is there to be tapped by all women who do not fear the revelation of connection to themselves.

Have you read my work, and the work of other Black women, for what it could give you? Or did you hunt through only to find words that would legitimize your chapter on African genital mutilation in the eyes of other Black women? And if so, then why not use our words to legitimize or illustrate the other places where we connect in our being and becoming? If, on the other hand, it was not Black women you were attempting to reach, in what way did our words illustrate your point for white women?

Mary, I ask that you be aware of how this serves the destructive forces of racism and separation between women − the assumption that the herstory and myth of white women is the legitimate and sole herstory and myth of all women to call upon for power and background, and that nonwhite women and our herstories are noteworthy only as decorations, or examples of female victimization. I ask that you be aware of the effect that this dismissal has upon the community of Black women and other women of Color, and how it devalues your own words. This dismissal does not essentially differ from the specialized devaluations that make Black women prey, for instance, to the murders even now happening in your own city. When patriarchy dismisses us, it encourages our murderers. When radical lesbian feminist theory dismisses us, it encourages its own demise.

This dismissal stands as a real block to communication between us. This block makes it far easier to turn away from you completely than to attempt to understand the thinking behind your choices. Should the next step be war between us, or separation? Assimilation within a solely western european herstory is not acceptable.

Mary, I ask that you re-member what is dark and ancient and divine within yourself that aids your speaking. As outsiders, we need each other for support and connection and all the other necessities of living on the borders. But in order to come together we must recognize each other. Yet I feel that since you have so completely un-recognized me, perhaps I have been in error concerning you and no longer recognize you.

I feel you do celebrate differences between white women as a creative force toward change, rather than a reason for misunderstanding and separation. But you fail to recognize that, as women, those differences expose all women to various forms and degrees of patriarchal oppression, some of which we share and some of which we do not. For instance, surely you know that for nonwhite women in this country, there is an 80 percent fatality rate from breast cancer; three times the number of unnecessary eventrations, hysterectomies and sterilizations as for white women; three times as many chances of being raped, murdered, or assaulted as exist for white women. These are statistical facts, not coincidences nor paranoid fantasies.

Within the community of women, racism is a reality force in my life as it is not in yours. The white women with hoods on in Ohio handing out KKK literature on the street may not like what you have to say, but they will shoot me on sight. (If you and I were to walk into a classroom of women in Dismal Gulch, Alabama, where the only thing they knew about each of us was that we were both Lesbian/Radical/Feminist, you would see exactly what I mean.)

The oppression of women knows no ethnic nor racial boundaries, true, but that does not mean it is identical within those differences. Nor do the reservoirs of our ancient power know these boundaries. To deal with one without even alluding to the other is to distort our commonality as well as our difference.

For then beyond sisterhood is still racism.

We first met at the MLA panel, "The Transformation of Silence Into Language and Action." This letter attempts to break a silence which I had imposed upon myself shortly before that date. I had decided never again to speak to white women about racism. I felt it was wasted energy because of destructive guilt and defensiveness, and because whatever I had to say might better be said by white women to one another at far less emotional cost to the speaker, and probably with a better hearing. But I would like not to destroy you in my consciousness, not to have to. So as a sister Hag, I ask you to speak to my perceptions.

Whether or not you do, Mary, again I thank you for what I have learned from you.

This letter is in repayment.

In the hands of Afrekete,
Audre Lorde

Man Child: A Black Lesbian Feminist's Response*

THIS ARTICLE IS NOT a theoretical discussion of Lesbian Mothers and their Sons, nor a how-to article. It is an attempt to scrutinize and share some pieces of that common history belonging to my son and to me. I have two children: a fifteen-and-a-half-year-old daughter Beth, and a fourteen-year-old son Jonathan. This is the way it was/is with me and Jonathan, and I leave the theory to another time and person. This is one woman's telling.

I have no golden message about the raising of sons for other lesbian mothers, no secret to transpose your questions into certain light. I have my own ways of rewording those same questions, hoping we will all come to speak those questions and pieces of our lives we need to share. We are women making contact within ourselves and with each other across the restrictions of a printed page, bent upon the use of our own/one another's knowledges.

The truest direction comes from inside. I give the most strength to my children by being willing to look within myself, and by being honest with them about what I find there, without expecting a response beyond their years. In this way they begin to learn to look beyond their own fears.

* First published in *Conditions: Four* (1979).

All our children are outriders for a queendom not yet assured.

My adolescent son's growing sexuality is a conscious dynamic between Jonathan and me. It would be presumptuous of me to discuss Jonathan's sexuality here, except to state my belief that whomever he chooses to explore this area with, his choices will be nonoppressive, joyful, and deeply felt from within, places of growth.

One of the difficulties in writing this piece has been temporal; this is the summer when Jonathan is becoming a man, physically. And our sons must become men — such men as we hope our daughters, born and unborn, will be pleased to live among. Our sons will not grow into women. Their way is more difficult than that of our daughters, for they must move away from us, without us. Hopefully, our sons have what they have learned from us, and a howness to forge it into their own image.

Our daughters have us, for measure or rebellion or outline or dream; but the sons of lesbians have to make their own definitions of self as men. This is both power and vulnerability. The sons of lesbians have the advantage of our blueprints for survival, but they must take what we know and transpose it into their own maleness. May the goddess be kind to my son, Jonathan.

Recently I have met young Black men about whom I am pleased to say that their future and their visions, as well as their concerns within the present, intersect more closely with Jonathan's than do my own. I have shared vision with these men as well as temporal strategies for our survivals and I appreciate the spaces in which we could sit down together. Some of these men I met at the First Annual Conference of Third World Lesbians and Gays held in Washington D.C. in October, 1979. I have met others in different places and do not know how they identify themselves sexually. Some of these men are raising families alone. Some have adopted sons. They are Black men who dream and who act and who own their feelings, questioning. It is heartening to know our sons do not step out alone.

When Jonathan makes me angriest, I always say he is bringing out the testosterone in me. What I mean is that he is representing some piece of myself as a woman that I am reluctant to acknowledge or explore. For instance, what does "acting like a man" mean? For me, what I reject? For Jonathan, what he is trying to redefine?

Raising Black children — female and male — in the mouth of a racist, sexist, suicidal dragon is perilous and chancy. If they cannot love and resist at the same time, they will probably not survive. And in order to survive they must let go. This is what mothers teach — love, survival — that is, self-definition and letting go. For each of these, the ability to feel strongly and to recognize those feelings is central: how to feel love, how to neither discount fear nor be overwhelmed by it, how to enjoy feeling deeply.

I wish to raise a Black man who will not be destroyed by, nor settle for, those corruptions called *power* by the white fathers who mean his destruction as surely as they mean mine. I wish to raise a Black man who will recognize that the legitimate objects of his hostility are not women, but the particulars of a structure that programs him to fear and despise women as well as his own Black self.

For me, this task begins with teaching my son that I do not exist to do his feeling for him.

Men who are afraid to feel must keep women around to do their feeling for them while dismissing us for the same supposedly "inferior" capacity to feel deeply. But in this way also, men deny themselves their own essential humanity, becoming trapped in dependency and fear.

As a Black woman committed to a liveable future, and as a mother loving and raising a boy who will become a man, I must examine all my possibilities of being within such a destructive system.

Jonathan was three-and-one-half when Frances, my lover, and I met; he was seven when we all began to live together permanently. From the start, Frances' and my insistence that there be no secrets in our household about the fact that we were lesbians has been the source of problems and strengths for both children. In the beginning, this insistence grew out of the knowledge, on both our parts, that whatever was hidden out of fear could always be used either against the children or ourselves — one imperfect but useful argument for honesty. The knowledge of fear can help make us free.

> for the embattled
> there is no place
> that cannot be
> home
> nor is.*

For survival, Black children in america must be raised to be warriors. For survival, they must also be raised to recognize the enemy's many faces. Black children of lesbian couples have an advantage because they learn, very early, that oppression comes in many different forms, none of which have anything to do with their own worth.

To help give me perspective, I remember that for years, in the namecalling at school, boys shouted at Jonathan not — "your mother's a lesbian" — but rather — "your mother's a nigger."

When Jonathan was eight years old and in the third grade we moved, and he went to a new school where his life was hellish as a new boy on the block. He did not like to play rough games. He did not like to fight. He did not like to stone dogs. And all this marked him early on as an easy target.

When he came in crying one afternoon, I heard from Beth how the corner bullies were making Johathan wipe their shoes on the way home whenever Beth wasn't there to fight them off. And when I heard that the ringleader was a little boy in Jonathan's class his own size, an interesting and very disturbing thing happened to me.

My fury at my own long-ago impotence, and my present pain at his suffering, made me start to forget all that I knew about violence and fear, and blaming the victim, I started to hiss at the weeping child. "The next time you come in here crying . . . ," and I suddenly caught myself in horror.

This is the way we allow the destruction of our sons to begin — in the name of protection and to ease our own pain. My son get beaten up? I was about to demand that he buy that first

* From "School Note" in *The Black Unicorn* (W.W. Norton and Company, New York, 1978), p. 55.

lesson in the corruption of power, that might makes right. I could hear myself beginning to perpetuate the age-old distortions about what strength and bravery really are.

And no, Jonathan didn't have to fight if he didn't want to, but somehow he did have to feel better about not fighting. An old horror rolled over me of being the fat kid who ran away, terrified of getting her glasses broken.

About that time a very wise woman said to me, "Have you ever told Jonathan that once you used to be afraid, too?"

The idea seemed far-out to me at the time, but the next time he came in crying and sweaty from having run away again, I could see that he felt shamed at having failed me, or some image he and I had created in his head of mother/woman. This image of woman being able to handle it all was bolstered by the fact that he lived in a household with three strong women, his lesbian parents and his forthright older sister. At home, for Jonathan, power was clearly female.

And because our society teaches us to think in an either/or mode — kill or be killed, dominate or be dominated — this meant that he must either surpass or be lacking. I could see the implications of this line of thought. Consider the two western classic myth/models of mother/son relationships: Jocasta/Oedipus, the son who fucks his mother, and Clytemnestra/Orestes, the son who kills his mother.

It all felt connected to me.

I sat down on the hallway steps and took Jonathan on my lap and wiped his tears. "Did I ever tell you about how I used to be afraid when I was your age?"

I will never forget the look on that little boy's face as I told him the tale of my glasses and my after-school fights. It was a look of relief and total disbelief, all rolled into one.

It is as hard for our children to believe that we are not omnipotent as it is for us to know it, as parents. But that knowledge is necessary as the first step in the reassessment of power as something other than might, age, privilege, or the lack of fear. It is an important step for a boy, whose societal destruction begins when he is forced to believe that he can only be strong if he doesn't feel, or if he wins.

I thought about all this one year later when Beth and Jonathan, ten and nine, were asked by an interviewer how they thought they had been affected by being children of a feminist.

Jonathan said that he didn't think there was too much in feminism for boys, although it certainly was good to be able to cry if he felt like it and not to have to play football if he didn't want to. I think of this sometimes now when I see him practising for his Brown Belt in Tae Kwon Do.

The strongest lesson I can teach my son is the same lesson I teach my daughter: how to be who he wishes to be for himself. And the best way I can do this is to be who I am and hope that he will learn from this not how to be me, which is not possible, but how to be himself. And this means how to move to that voice from within himself, rather than to those raucous, persuasive, or threatening voices from outside, pressuring him to be what the world wants him to be.

And that is hard enough.

Jonathan is learning to find within himself some of the different faces of courage and strength, whatever he chooses to call them. Two years ago, when Jonathan was twelve and in the seventh grade, one of his friends at school who had been to the house persisted in calling Frances "the maid." When Jonathan corrected him, the boy then referred to her as "the cleaning woman." Finally Jonathan said, simply, "Frances is not the cleaning woman, she's my mother's lover." Interestingly enough, it is the teachers at this school who still have not recovered from his openness.

Frances and I were considering attending a Lesbian/Feminist conference this summer, when we were notified that no boys over ten were allowed. This presented logistic as well as philosophical problems for us, and we sent the following letter:

Sisters:

Ten years as an interracial lesbian couple has taught us both the dangers of an oversimplified approach to the nature and solutions of any oppression, as well as the danger inherent in an incomplete vision.

Our thirteen-year-old son represents as much hope for our future world as does our fifteen-year-old daughter, and we are not willing to abandon him to the killing streets of New York City while we journey west to help form a Lesbian-Feminist vision of the future world in which we can all survive and flourish. I hope we can continue this dialogue in the near future, as I feel it is important to our vision and our survival.

The question of separatism is by no means simple. I am thankful that one of my children is male, since that helps to keep me honest. Every line I write shrieks there are no easy solutions.

I grew up in largely female environments, and I know how crucial that has been to my own development. I feel the want and need often for the society of women, exclusively. I recognize that our own spaces are essential for developing and recharging.

As a Black woman, I find it necessary to withdraw into all-Black groups at times for exactly the same reasons — differences in stages of development and differences in levels of interaction. Frequently, when speaking with men and white women, I am reminded of how difficult and time-consuming it is to have to reinvent the pencil every time you want to send a message.

But this does not mean that my responsibility for my son's education stops at age ten, any more than it does for my daughter's. However, for each of them, that responsibility does grow less and less as they become more woman and man.

Both Beth and Jonathan need to know what they can share and what they cannot, how they are joined and how they are not. And Frances and I, as grown women and lesbians coming more and more into our power, need to relearn the experience that difference does not have to be threatening.

When I envision the future, I think of the world I crave for my daughters and my sons. It is thinking for survival of the species — thinking for life.

Most likely there will always be women who move with women, women who live with men, men who choose men. I work for a time when women with women, women with men, men with men, all share the work of a world that does not barter bread or self for obedience, nor beauty, nor love. And in that world we will raise our children free to choose how best to fulfill themselves. For we are jointly responsible for the care and raising of the young, since *that* they be raised is a function, ultimately, of the species.

Within that tripartite pattern of relating/existence, the raising of the young will be the joint responsibility of all adults who choose to be associated with children. Obviously, the children raised within each of these three relationships will be different, lending a special savor to that eternal inquiry into how best can we live our lives.

Jonathan was three-and-a-half when Frances and I met. He is now fourteen years old. I feel the living perspective that having lesbian parents has brought to Jonathan is a valuable addition to his human sensitivity.

Jonathan has had the advantage of growing up within a nonsexist relationship, one in which this society's pseudo-natural assumptions of ruler/ruled are being challenged. And this is not only because Frances and I are lesbians, for unfortunately there are some lesbians who are still locked into patriarchal patterns of unequal power relationships.

These assumptions of power relationships are being questioned because Frances and I, often painfully and with varying degrees of success, attempt to evaluate and measure over and over again our feelings concerning power, our own and others'. And we explore with care those areas concerning how it is used and expressed between us and between us and the children, openly and otherwise. A good part of our biweekly family meetings are devoted to this exploration.

As parents, Frances and I have given Jonathan our love, our openness, and our dreams to help form his visions. Most importantly, as the son of lesbians, he has had an invaluable model — not only of a relationship — but of relating.

Jonathan is fourteen now. In talking over this paper with him and asking his permission to share some pieces of his life, I asked Jonathan what he felt were the strongest negative and the strongest positive aspects for him in having grown up with lesbian parents.

He said the strongest benefit he felt he had gained was that he knew a lot more about people than most other kids his age that he knew, and that he did not have a lot of the hang-ups that some other boys did about men and women.

And the most negative aspect he felt, Jonathan said, was the ridicule he got from some kids with straight parents.

"You mean, from your peers?" I said.

"Oh no," he answered promptly. "My peers know better. I mean other kids."

An Interview: Audre Lorde and Adrienne Rich*

Adrienne: What do you mean when you say that two essays, "Poetry Is Not a Luxury" and "Uses of the Erotic" are really progressions?

Audre: They're part of something that's not finished yet. I don't know what the rest of it is, but they're clear progressions in feeling out something connected with the first piece of prose I ever wrote. One thread in my life is the battle to preserve my perceptions — pleasant or unpleasant, painful or whatever . . .

Adrienne: And however much they were denied.

Audre: And however painful some of them were. When I think of the way in which I courted punishment, just swam into it: "If this is the only way you're going to deal with me, you're gonna have to deal with me this way."

Adrienne: You're talking about as a young child?

Audre: I'm talking about throughout my life. I kept myself through feeling. I lived through it. And at such a subterranean level that I didn't know how to talk. I was busy feeling out other ways of getting and giving information and whatever else I could because talking wasn't where it was at. People were talking

* This interview, held on August 30, 1979 in Montague, Massachusetts, was edited from three hours of tapes we made together. It was commissioned by Marilyn Hacker, the guest editor of *Woman Poet: The East* (Women-In-Literature, Reno, Nevada, 1981), where a portion of it appears. The interview was first published in *Signs*, vol. 6, no. 4 (Summer 1981).

all around me all the time — and not either getting or giving much that was useful to them or to me.

Adrienne: And not listening to what you tried to say, if you did speak.

Audre: When you asked how I began writing, I told you how poetry functioned specifically for me from the time I was very young. When someone said to me, "How do you feel?" or "What do you think?" or asked another direct question, I would recite a poem, and somewhere in that poem would be the feeling, the vital piece of information. It might be a line. It might be an image. The poem was my response.

Adrienne; Like a translation into this poem that already existed of something you knew in a preverbal way. So the poem became your language?

Audre: Yes. I remember reading in the children's room of the library, I couldn't have been past the second or third grade, but I remember the book. It was illustrated by Arthur Rackham, a book of poems. These were old books; the library in Harlem used to get the oldest books, in the worst condition. Walter de la Mare's "The Listeners" — I will never forget that poem.

Adrienne: Where the traveler rides up to the door of the empty house?

Audre: That's right. He knocks at the door and nobody answers. " 'Is there anybody there?' he said." That poem imprinted itself on me. And finally, he's beating down the door and nobody answers, and he has a feeling that there really is somebody in there. Then he turns his horse and says, " 'Tell them I came, and nobody answered. That I kept my word.' " I used to recite that poem to myself all the time. It was one of my favorites. And if you'd asked me, "What is it about?" I don't think I could have told you. But this was the first reason for my own writing, my need to say things I couldn't say otherwise when I couldn't find other poems to serve.

Adrienne: You had to make your own.

Audre: There were so many complex emotions for which poems did not exist. I had to find a secret way to express my feelings. I used to memorize my poems. I would say them out; I didn't use to write them down. I had this long fund of poetry in my head. And I remember trying when I was in high school not to think in poems. I saw the way other people thought, and it was an amazement to me — step by step, not in bubbles up from chaos that you had to anchor with words . . . I really do believe I learned this from my mother.

Adrienne: Learned what from your mother?

Audre: The important value of nonverbal communication, beneath language. My life depended on it. At the same time, living in the world, I didn't want to have anything to do with the way she was using language. My mother had a strange way with words: if one didn't serve her or wasn't strong enough, she'd just make up another word, and then that would enter our family language forever, and woe betide any of us who forgot it. But I think I got another message from her . . . that there was a whole powerful world of nonverbal communication and contact between people that was absolutely essential and that was what you had to learn to decipher and use. One of the reasons I had so much trouble growing up was that my parents, my mother in particular, always expected me to know what she was feeling and what she expected me to do without telling me. And I thought this was natural. My mother would expect me to know things, whether or not she spoke them . . .

Adrienne: Ignorance of the law was no excuse.

Audre: That's right. It's very confusing. But eventually I learned how to acquire vital and protective information without words. My mother used to say to me, "Don't just listen like a ninny to what people say in their mouth." But then she'd proceed to say something that didn't feel right to me. You always learned from observing. You have to pick things up nonverbally because people will never tell you what you're supposed to know. You have to get it for yourself, whatever it is that you need in order to survive. And if you make a mistake you get punished for it, but that's no big thing. You become strong by doing the things you need to be strong for. This is the way genuine learning takes place. That's a very difficult way to live, but it also has served me. It's been an asset as well as a liability. When I went to high school, I found out that people really thought in different ways — perceived, puzzled out, acquired information verbally. I had such a hard time. I never studied; I literally intuited all my teachers. That's why it was so important to get a teacher who I liked because I never studied, I never read my assignment, and I would get all this stuff — what they felt, what they knew — but I missed a lot of other stuff, a lot of my own original workings.

Adrienne: When you said you never read, you meant you never read the assignments, but you were reading?

Audre: If I read things that were assigned, I didn't read them the way we were supposed to. Everything was like a poem, with different curves, different levels. So I always felt that the ways I took things in were different from the ways other people took them in. I used to practice trying to think.

Adrienne: That thing those other people presumably did. Do you remember what that was like?

Audre: Yes. I had an image of trying to reach something around a corner, that it was just eluding me. The image was constantly vanishing. There was an experience I had in Mexico, when I moved to Cuernavaca . . .

Adrienne: This was when you were about how old?

Audre: I was nineteen. I was commuting to Mexico City for classes. In order to get to my early class I would catch a six o'clock turismo in the village plaza. I would come out of my house before dawn. You know, there are two volcanoes, Popocatepetl and Ixtacuhuatl. I thought they were clouds the first time I saw them through my windows. It would be dark, and I would see the snow on top of the mountains and the sun coming up. And when the sun crested, at a certain point, the birds would start. But because we were in the valley it would still look like night. But there would be the light of the snow. And then this incredible crescendo of birds. One morning I came over the hill and the green, wet smells came up. And then the birds, the sound of them I'd never really noticed, never heard birds before. I was walking down the hill and I was transfixed. It was very beautiful. I hadn't been writing all the time I was in Mexico. And poetry was the thing I had with words, that was so important . . . And on that hill, I had the first intimation that I could bring those two together. I could infuse words directly with what I was feeling. I didn't have to create the world I wrote about. I realized that words could tell. That there was such a thing as an emotional sentence. Until then, I would make these constructs and somewhere in there would be a nugget, like a Chinese bun, a piece of nourishment, the thing I really needed, which I had to create. There on that hill, I was filled with the smell and feeling and the way it looked, filled with such beauty that I could not believe . . . I had always fantasized it before. I used to fantasize trees and dream forest. Until I got spectacles when I was four I thought trees were green clouds. When I read Shakespeare in high school, I would get off on his gardens and Spanish moss and roses and trellises with beautiful women at rest and sun on red brick. When I was in Mexico I found out this could be a reality. And I learned that day on the mountain that words can match that, re-create it.

Adrienne: Do you think that in Mexico you were seeing a reality as extraordinary and vivid and sensual as you had been fantasizing it could be?

Audre: I think so. I had always thought I had to do it in my head, make it up. I learned in Mexico that you can't even make it up unless it happens, or can happen. Where it happened first for me I don't know; I do remember stories my mother would tell us about Grenada in the West Indies, where she was born . . . But that morning in Mexico I realized I did not have to make beauty up for the rest of my life. I remember trying to tell Eudora about this epiphany, and I didn't have the words for it. And I remember her saying, "Write a poem." When I tried to write a poem about the way I felt that morning, I could not do it, and all I had was the memory that there must be a way. That was incredibly important. I know that I came back from Mexico very, very different, and much of it had to do with what I learned from Eudora. But more than that, it was a kind of releasing of my work, a releasing of myself.

Adrienne: Then you went back to the Lower East Side, right?

Audre: Yes, I went back to living with my friend Ruth, and I began trying to get a job. I had had a year of college, but I could not function in those people's world. So I thought I could be a nurse. And I was having such a hard time getting any kind of work. I felt, well, a Practical Nursing license, and then I'll go back to Mexico . . .

Adrienne: With my trade.

Audre: But that wasn't possible either. I didn't have any money, and Black women were not given Practical Nursing fellowships. I didn't realize it at the time because what they said was that my eyes were too bad. But the first thing I did when I came back was to write a piece of prose about Mexico, called "La Llorona." La Llorona is a legend in that part of Mexico, around Cuernavaca. You know Cuernavaca? You know the big barrancas? When the rains come to the mountains, the boulders rush through the big ravines. The sound, the first rush, would start one or two days before the rains came. All the rocks tumbling down from the mountains made a voice, and the echoes would resound and it would be a sound of weeping, with the waters behind it. Modesta, a woman who lived in the house, told me the legend of La Llorona. A woman had three sons and found her husband lying in another woman's bed — it's the Medea story — and drowned her sons in the barrancas, drowned her children. And every year around this time she comes back to mourn the deaths. I took this story and out of a combination of ways I was feeling I wrote a story called "La Llorona." It's a story essentially of my mother and me. It was as if I had picked my mother up and put her in that place: here is this woman who kills, who wants something, the woman who consumes her children, who wants too much, but wants not because she's evil but because she wants her own life, but by now it is so distorted. . . . It was a very strange unfinished story, but the dynamic . . .

Adrienne: It sounds like you were trying to pull those two pieces of your life together, your mother and what you'd learned in Mexico.

Audre: Yes. You see, I didn't deal at all with how strong my mother was inside of me, but she was, nor with how involved I was. But this story is beautiful. Pieces of it are in my head where the poetry pool is, phrases and so on. I had never written prose before and I've never written any since until just now. I published it under the name *Rey Domini* in a magazine . . .

Adrienne: Why did you use a pseudonym?

Audre: Because . . . I don't write stories. I write poetry. So I had to put it under another name.

Adrienne: Because it was a different piece of you?

Audre: That's right. I only write poetry and here is this story. But I used the name *Rey Domini*, which is *Audre Lorde* in Latin.

Adrienne: Did you really not write prose from the time of that story until a couple of years ago, when you wrote "Poetry Is Not a Luxury"?

Audre: I couldn't. For some reason, the more poetry I wrote, the less I felt I could write prose. Someone would ask for a book review, or, when I worked at the library, for a precis about books — it wasn't that I didn't have the skills. I knew about sentences by that time. I knew how to construct a paragraph. But communicating deep feeling in linear, solid blocks of print felt arcane, a method beyond me.

Adrienne: But you'd been writing letters like wildfire, hadn't you?

Audre: Well, I didn't write letters as such. I wrote stream of consciousness, and for people who were close enough to me this would serve. My friends gave me back the letters I wrote them from Mexico — strange, those are the most formed. I remember feeling I could not focus on a thought long enough to have it from start to finish, but I could ponder a poem for days, camp out in its world.

Adrienne: Do you think that was because you still had this idea that thinking was a mysterious process that other people did and that you had to sort of practice? That it wasn't something you just did?

Audre: It was a very mysterious process for me. And it was one I had come to suspect because I had seen so many errors committed in its name, and I had come not to respect it. On the other hand, I was also afraid of it because there were inescapable conclusions or convictions I had come to about my own life, my own feelings, that defied thought. And I wasn't going to let them go. I wasn't going to give them up. They were too precious to me. They were life to me. But I couldn't analyze or understand them because they didn't make the kind of sense I had been taught to expect through understanding. There were things I knew and couldn't say. And I couldn't understand them.

Adrienne: In the sense of being able to take them out, analyze them, defend them?

Audre: . . . write prose about them. Right. I wrote a lot of those poems you first knew me by, those poems in *The First Cities,** way back in high school. If you had asked me to talk about one of those poems, I'd have talked in the most banal way. All I had was the sense that I had to hold on to these feelings and that I had to air them in some way.

Adrienne: But they were also being transformed into language.

Audre: That's right. When I wrote something that finally had it, I would say it aloud and it would come alive, become real. It would start repeating itself and I'd know, that's struck, that's true. Like a bell. Something struck true. And there the words would be.

Adrienne: How do you feel writing connected for you with teaching?

Audre: I know teaching is a survival technique. It is for me and I think it is in general; the only way real learning happens. Because I myself was learning something I needed to continue living. And I was examining it and teaching it at the same time I was learning it. I was teaching it to myself aloud. And it started out at Tougaloo in a poetry workshop.

Adrienne: You were ill when you were called to go down to Tougaloo?

Audre: Yes, I felt . . . I had almost died.

Adrienne: What was going on?

Audre: Diane di Prima — that was 1967 — had started the Poets Press. And she said, "You know, it's time you had a book." And I said, "Well, who's going to print it?" I was going to put those poems away because I found I was revising too much instead of writing new poems, and that's how I found out, again

---

* *The First Cities* (Poets Press, New York, 1968).

through experience, that poetry is not Play-Doh. You can't take a poem and keep re-forming it. It is itself, and you have to know how to cut it, and if there's something else you want to say, that's fine. But I was repolishing and repolishing, and Diane said, "You have to print these. Put 'em out." And the Poets Press published *The First Cities*. Well, I worked on that book, getting it together, and it was going into press . . . I had gotten the proofs back and I started repolishing again and realized, "This is going to be a book!" Putting myself on the line. People I don't even know are going to read these poems. What's going to happen?

It felt very critical, and I was in an absolute blaze of activity because things were so bad at home financially. I went out and got a job; I was with the two kids in the daytime and worked at the library at night. Jonathan used to cry every night when I left, and I would hear his shrieks going down this long hall to the elevator. I was working nights, and I'd apprenticed myself to a stained-glass window-maker, and I was working in my mother's office, and making Christmas for my friends, and I became very ill — I had overdone it. I was too sick to get up, and Ed answered the phone. It was Galen Williams from the Poetry Center asking if I'd like to go as poet-in-residence to Tougaloo, a Black college in Mississippi. I'd been recommended for a grant. It was Ed who said, "You have to do this." My energy was at such a low ebb that I couldn't see how. It was very frightening to me, the idea of someone responding to me as a poet. This book, by the way, hadn't even come out yet, you understand?

Adrienne: And suddenly you were already being taken seriously by unseen people out there.

Audre: That's right. In particular, I was asked to be public; to speak *as*, rather than *to*. But I felt as if I'd come back from the dead at that point, and so everything was up for grabs. I thought, hey, very good, let's see — not because I felt I could do it, I just knew it was new and different. I was terrified to go south. Then there were echoes of an old dream: I had wanted to go to Tougaloo years before. My friend Elaine and I were going to join the Freedom Riders in Jackson when we left California in 1961 to return to New York, and Elaine's mother got down on her knees in San Francisco and begged us please not to do this, that they would kill us, and we didn't do it. So going to Tougaloo in Jackson was part of the mythic . . .

Adrienne: But it sounds as if earlier you had been more romantic about what going south would mean, and six years later, with two kids and everything that had happened in between in the south . . .

Audre: I was scared. I thought: "I'm going." Really, it was the first thing that countered the fury and pain I felt at leaving that little boy screaming every night. It was like — all right, if I can walk out and hear that child screaming in order to go down to the library and work every night, then I'm gonna be able at least to do something that I want to find out about. So I went.

Adrienne: Were you scared at Tougaloo, in terms of teaching, meeting your first workshop?

Audre: Yes, but it was a nurturing atmosphere. I lived there for two weeks before I went around really gathering people, and there were eight students who were already writing poetry. The ways in which I was on the line in Tougaloo . . . I began to learn about courage, I began to learn to talk. This was a small group and we became very close. I learned so much from listening to people. The only thing I had was honesty and openness. And it was absolutely necessary for me to declare, as terrified as I was, as we were opening to each other, "The father of my children is white." And what that meant in Tougaloo to those young Black people then, to talk about myself openly and deal with their hostility, their sense of disillusionment, to come past that, was very hard.

Adrienne: It must have been particularly hard since you knew by then that the marriage was going nowhere. It's like having to defend something that was not in itself defensible.

Audre: What I was defending was something that needed defense. And this moved it out of "I'm defending Ed because I want to live with him." It was, "I'm defending this relationship because we have a right to examine it and try it." So there's the northern Black poet making contact with these young southern Black people who are not saying, "This is what we need you for," but were telling me by who they were what they needed from me. In the poem "Black Studies"* a lot of that starts coming through. Tougaloo laid the foundation for that poem, that knowledge born five years later. My students needed my perception, yet my perception of their need was different from what they were saying. What they were saying aloud was, "We need strong Black people," but what they were also saying was that their ideas of what strong was had come from our oppressors and didn't jibe with their feelings at all.

It was through poetry that we began to deal with these things — formally. I knew nothing. Adrienne, I had never read a book about poetry! I picked up one day a book by Karl Shapiro, a little thin white book. I opened it and something he said made sense. "Poetry doesn't sell Cadillacs." It was the first time I'd ever talked about writing; always before I'd listened — part of my being inarticulate, inscrutable; I didn't understand in terms of verbalization, and if I did I was too terrified to speak anyway. But at Tougaloo we talked about poetry. And I got the first copies of my book there at Tougaloo.

I had never been in this relationship with Black people before. Never. There had been a very uneasy dialogue between me and the Harlem Writers' Guild where I felt I was tolerated but never really accepted — that I was both crazy and queer but would grow out of it all. Johnny Clarke adopted me because he really loved me, and he's a kind man. And he taught me wonderful things about Africa. And he said to me, "You are a poet. You are a poet. I don't understand your poetry but you are a poet, you are." So I would get this underlining of me. "You're not doing what you're supposed to do, but, yes, you can do it and we totally expect you to. You are a bright and shining light. You're off on a lot of wrong turns — women, the Village, white people, all of this, but you're young yet. You'll find your way." So I would get these double messages, this kind of underlining and rejection at the same time. It reduplicated my family, you see. In my family it was: "You're a Lorde, so that makes you special and particular above anybody else in the world. But you're not our kind of Lorde, so when are you going to straighten out and act right?"

* *New York Head Shop and Museum* (Broadside Press, Detroit, 1974), pp. 52-56.

Adrienne: And did you feel, there in the Harlem Writers' Guild, the same kind of unwritten laws that you had to figure out in order to do right?

Audre: Yes, I would bring poems to read at the meetings. And hoping, well, they're gonna tell me actually what it is they want, but they never could, never did.

Adrienne: Were there women in that group, older women?

Audre: Rosa Guy was older than I, but she was still very young. I remember only one other woman, Gertrude McBride. But she came in and out of the workshop so quickly I never knew her. For the most part, the men were the core. My friend Jeannie and I were members but in a slightly different position; we were in high school.

Adrienne: And so Tougaloo was an entirely different experience of working with other Black writers.

Audre: When I went to Tougaloo, I didn't know what to give or where it was going to come from. I knew I couldn't give what regular teachers of poetry give, nor did I want to, because they'd never served me. I couldn't give what English teachers give. The only thing I had to give was me. And I was so involved with these young people — I really loved them. I knew the emotional life of each of those students because we would have conferences, and that became inseparable from their poetry. I would talk to them in the group about their poetry in terms of what I knew about their lives, and that there was a real connection between the two that was inseparable no matter what they'd been taught to the contrary.

I knew by the time I left Tougaloo that teaching was the work I needed to be doing, that library work — by this time I was head librarian at the Town School — was not enough. It had been very satisfying to me. And I had a kind of stature I hadn't had before in terms of working. But from the time I went to Tougaloo and did that workshop, I knew: not only, yes, I am a poet, but also, this is the kind of work I'm going to do.

Practically all the poems in *Cables to Rage** I wrote in Tougaloo. I was there for six weeks. I came back knowing that my relationship with Ed was not enough: either we were going to

---

* *Cables to Rage* (Paul Breman, Heritage Series, London, 1970).

change it or end it. I didn't know how to end it because there had never been any endings for me. But I had met Frances at Tougaloo, and I knew she was going to be a permanent person in my life. However, I didn't know how we were going to work it out. I'd left a piece of my heart in Tougaloo not just because of Frances but because of what my students there had taught me.

And I came back, and my students called me and told me — they were all of them also in the Tougaloo choir — they were coming to New York to sing in Carnegie Hall with Duke Ellington on April 4, and I covered it for the *Clarion-Ledger*, in Jackson, so I was there, and while we were there Martin Luther King was killed.

Adrienne: On that night?

Audre: I was with the Tougaloo choir at Carnegie Hall when he was killed. They were singing "What the World Needs Now Is Love." And they interrupted it to tell us that Martin Luther King had been killed.

Adrienne: What did people do?

Audre: Duke Ellington started to cry. Honeywell, the head of the choir, said, "The only thing we can do here is finish this as a memorial." And they sang again, "What the World Needs Now is Love." The kids were crying. The audience was crying. And then the choir stopped. They cut the rest of it short. But they sang that song and it kept reverberating. It was more than pain. The horror, the enormity of what was happening. Not just the death of King, but what it meant. I have always had the sense of Armageddon and it was much stronger in those days, the sense of living on the edge of chaos. Not just personally, but on the world level. That we were dying, that we were killing our world — that sense had always been with me. That whatever I was doing, whatever we were doing that was creative and right, functioned to hold us from going over the edge. That this was the most we could do while we constructed some saner future. But that we were in that kind of peril. And here it was reality, in fact. Some of the poems — "Equinox"* is one of them — come

---

* First published in *From a Land Where Other People Live* (Broadside Press, Detroit, 1973), and collected in *Chosen Poems: Old and New* (W.W. Norton and Company, New York, 1982), pp. 39-40.

from then. I knew then that I had to leave the library. And it was just about this time that Yolanda took my book, *The First Cities*, to Mina Shaughnessy* who had been her teacher, and I think she said to Mina, "Why don't you have her teach?" — because that's the way, you know, Yolanda is.

Adrienne: But also, Mina would have listened to that.

Audre: So Yolanda came home and said, "Hey, the head of the SEEK** English program wants to meet you. Maybe you can get a job there." And I thought, I have to lay myself on the line. It's not going back south and being shot at, but when Mina said to me, "Teach," it was as threatening as that was. I felt at the time, I don't know how I'm gonna do it, but that's the front line for me. And I talked to Frances about this, because we'd had the Tougaloo experience, and I said, "If I could go to war, if I could pick up a gun to defend the things I believe, yes — but what am I gonna do in a classroom?" And Frances said, "You'll do just what you did at Tougaloo." And the first thing that I said to my SEEK students was, "I'm scared too."

Adrienne: I know I went in there in terror. But I went in white terror; you know, now you're on the line, all your racism is going to show . . .

Audre: I went in in Audre terror, Black terror. I thought, I have responsibility to these students. How am I going to speak to them? How am I going to tell them what I want from them — literally — that kind of terror. I did not know how to open my mouth and be understood. And my commadre, Yolanda, who was also a student in the SEEK program, said, "I guess you're just going to have to talk to them the same way you talk to me because I'm one of them and you've gotten across to me." I learned every single thing in every classroom. Every single class I ever walked into was like doing it anew. Every day, every week. But that was the exciting thing.

Adrienne: Did you teach English 1 — that back-to-back course where you could be a poet, a writing teacher, and not teach

---

* Mina Shaughnessy (1924-78), then director of the SEEK Writing Program at the City College, City University of New York.

** "Search for Education, Elevation, and Knowledge": A pre-baccalaureate program in compensatory education in the City University of New York in which a number of writer-teachers participated in the 1960s and early 1970s.

grammar, and they had an English instructor to teach the grammar? That was the only way I could have started doing it either.

Audre: I learned to teach grammar. And then I realized that we can't separate these two things. We have to do them together because they're integral. That's when I learned how important grammar is, that part of the understanding process is grammatical. That's how I taught myself to write prose. I kept learning and learning. I'd come into my class and say, "Guess what I found out last night. Tenses are a way of ordering the chaos around time." I learned that grammar was not arbitrary, that it served a purpose, that it helped to form the ways we thought, that it could be freeing as well as restrictive. And I sensed again how as children we learn this, and why. It's like driving a car: once we know it we can choose to discard it or use it, but you can't know if it has useful or destructive power until you have a handle on it. It's like fear: once you put your hand on it, you can use it or push it away. I was saying these things in class and dealing with what was happening with Frances and me, what was going on with this insane man I lived with who wanted to continue pretending life could be looked at one way and lived another. All this, every bit of it funneling into that class. My children were just learning to read in school, and that was important too because I could watch their processes. Then it got even heavier when I went up to Lehmann College and was teaching a class on racism in education, teaching these white students how it was, the connections between their lives and the fury . . .

Adrienne: You taught a course on racism for white students at Lehmann?

Audre: They were inaugurating a program in the Education Department for these white kids going into teaching in the New York City schools. Lehmann used to be 99 percent white, and it was these students coming out of the Education Department who were going to teach Black children in the city schools. So the course was called "Race and the Urban Situation." I had all these white students wanting to know, "What are we doing? Why are our kids hating us in the classroom?" I could not believe that they did not know the most elementary level of interactions. I would say, "When a white kid says 2 + 2 = 4, you say 'right.' In the same class, when a Black kid stands up and says 2 + 2 = 4, you pat him on the back, you say, 'Hey, that's wonderful.' But what message are you really giving? Or what happens when you walk down the street on your way to teach? When you walk into class? Let's play act a little." And all the fear and loathing of these young white college students would come pouring out; it had never been addressed.

Adrienne: They must have been mostly women, weren't they? In the Education Department?

Audre: Yes, mostly women, and they felt like unwilling sacrifices. But I began to feel by the end of two terms that there ought to be somebody white doing this. It was terribly costly emotionally. I didn't have more than one or two Black students in my class. One of them dropped out saying this wasn't right for him, and I thought, wait a minute, racism doesn't just distort white people — what about us? What about the effects of white racism upon the ways Black people view each other? Racism internalized? What about Black teachers going into ghetto schools? And I saw there were different problems, that were just as severe, for a Black teacher going into New York City schools after a racist, sexist education.

Adrienne: You mean in terms of expectations?

Audre: Not just in terms of expectations, but of self-image, in terms of confusion about loyalties. In terms of identifying with the oppressor. And I thought, who is going to start to deal with that? What do you do about it? This was where I wanted to use my energies. Meanwhile, this is 1969, and I'm thinking, what is my place in all this? There were two Black women in the class, and I tried to talk to them about us, as Black women, having to get together. The Black organizations on the campuses were revving up for the spring actions. And the women said, "You are insane, our men need us." It was a total rejection. "No, we can't come together as women. We're Black." But I had to keep trying to straighten out the threads because I knew the minute I stopped trying to straighten this shit out, it was going to engulf me. So the only hope I had was to work at it, work on all the threads. My love with Frances, Ed, the children, teaching Black students, the women.

And in '69 came the Black and Puerto Rican occupation at City College. Black students outside of class on the barricades. Yolanda and I would bring over soup and blankets and see Black women being fucked on tables and under desks. And while we'd be trying to speak to them as women, all we'd hear is, "The revolution is here, right?" Seeing how Black women were being used and abused was painful – putting those things together. I said, "I want to teach Black students again." I went to John Jay College and discussed a course with the dean on racism and the urban situation, and he said, "Come teach it." I taught two courses, that one and another new course I introduced to the English Department, which approached remedial writing through creative writing. It was confrontation teaching.

Adrienne: John Jay was largely a police college, right?

Audre: It had been a police college, but I began in 1970 after open admissions started, and John Jay was now a four-year senior college with a regular enrollment as well as an enrollment of City uniformed personnel. There were no Black teachers in English or history. Most of our incoming freshmen were Black or Puerto Rican. And my demeanor was very unthreatening.

Adrienne: I've seen your demeanor at John Jay and it was not unthreatening, but that was a bit later . . .

Audre: . . . and also, I was a Black woman. So then I came in and started this course and really meant business. And it was very heavily attended. A lot of Black and white policemen registered for it. And literally, I used to be terrified about the guns.

Adrienne: They were wearing guns?

Audre: Yes. And since open admissions made college accessible to all high school graduates, we had cops and kids off the block in the same class. In 1970, the Black Panthers were being murdered in Chicago. Here we had Black and white cops, and Black and white kids off the block. Most of the women were young, Black, together women who had come to college now because they'd not been able to get in before. Some of them were SEEK students, but not all, and this was the one chance for them. A lot of them were older. They were very streetwise, but they had done very little work with themselves as Black women. They had done it only in relation to, against, whitey. The enemy was always outside. I did that course in the same way I did all the others, which was learning as I went along, asking the hard questions, not knowing what was coming next. I wish I had recorded some of it. Like the young white cop in the class saying, "Yeah, but everybody needs someone to look down on, don't they?" By then I'd learned how to talk. Things weren't all concise or refined, but enough of it got through to them; their own processes would start. I came to realize that in one term that is the most you can do. There are people who can give chunks of information, perhaps, but that was not what I was about. The learning process is something you can incite, literally incite, like a riot. And then, just possibly, hopefully, it goes home, or on.

By that time the battle over the Black Studies Department had started at John Jay. And again I saw the use and abuse of women, of Black people, saw how Black studies was being used by the university in a really cynical fashion. A year later, I returned to the English Department. I had made a number of enemies. One of the attempts to discredit me among Black students was to say I was a lesbian. Now by this time I would have considered myself uncloseted, but I had never discussed my own poetry at John Jay, nor my sexuality. I knew, as I had always known, that the only way you can head people off from using who you are against you is to be honest and open first, to talk about yourself before they talk about you. It wasn't even courage. Speaking up was a protective mechanism for myself — like publishing "Love Poem" in Ms. magazine in 1971 and bringing it in and putting it up on the wall of the English Department.

Adrienne: I remember hearing you read "Love Poem" on the Upper West Side, a coffeehouse at 72nd Street. It was the first time I'd heard you read it. And I think it was about that time, the early seventies. You read it. It was incredible. Like defiance. It was glorious.

Audre: That's how I was feeling, back against the wall, because as bad as it is now, the idea of open lesbianism in the Black community was — I mean, we've moved miles in a very short time — totally horrible. My publisher called and literally said he didn't understand the words of "Love Poem." He said, "Now what is this all about? Are you supposed to be a man?" And he was a poet! And I said, "No, I'm a loving woman."

Adrienne: Well, don't tell me that your publisher had never heard of lesbians.

Audre: I'm sure he had, but the idea that I'd write a poem . . .

Adrienne: . . . That one of his poets in the Broadside Series . . .

Audre: That's right. And he was a sensitive man. He was a poet.

Adrienne: But he did print your work.

Audre: Yes, he did. But he didn't print that poem, the first time around. "Love Poem" was supposed to have been in *From a Land Where Other People Live.*

Adrienne: And it wasn't published in that book? You took it out?

Audre: Yes. But when you heard me read "Love Poem," I had already made up my mind that I wasn't going to be worrying any more over who knows and who doesn't know that I have always loved women. One thing has always kept me going — and it's not really courage or bravery, unless that's what courage or bravery is made of — is a sense that there are so many ways in which I'm vulnerable and cannot help but be vulnerable, I'm not going to be more vulnerable by putting weapons of silence in my enemies' hands. Being an open lesbian in the Black community is not easy, although being closeted is even harder.

When a people share a common oppression, certain kinds of skills and joint defenses are developed. And if you survive you survive because those skills and defenses have worked. When you come into conflict over other existing differences, there is a vulnerability to each other which is desperate and very deep. And that is what happens between Black men and women because we have certain weapons we have perfected together that white women and men have not shared. I said this to someone, and she said, very rightly, the same thing exists within the Jewish community between Jewish men and Jewish women. I think the oppression is different, but the same mechanism of vulnerability exists. When you share a common oppression you have certain additional weapons against each other because you've forged them in secret together against a common enemy. It's a fear that I'm still not free of and that I remember all the time when I deal with other Black women: the fear of the ex-comrade.

Adrienne: In "Poetry Is Not a Luxury," you wrote: "The white fathers told us, 'I think, therefore I am,' and the Black mother within each of us — the poet — whispers in our dreams, 'I feel, therefore I can be free.' " I've heard it remarked that here you are simply restating the old stereotype of the rational white male and the emotional dark female. I believe you were saying something very different, but could you talk a little about that?

Audre: I have heard that accusation, that I'm contributing to the stereotype, that I'm saying the province of intelligence and rationality belongs to the white male. But if you're traveling a road that begins nowhere and ends nowhere, the ownership of that road is meaningless. If you have no land out of which the road comes, no place that road goes to, geographically, no goal, then the existence of that road is totally meaningless. Leaving rationality to the white man is like leaving him a piece of that road that begins nowhere and ends nowhere. When I talk about the Black mother in each of us, the poet, I don't mean the Black mothers in each of us who are called poets, I mean the Black mother . . .

Adrienne: Who is the poet?

Audre: The Black mother who is the poet exists in every one of us. Now when males or patriarchal thinkers (whether male or female) reject that combination, then we're truncated. Rationality is not unnecessary. It serves the chaos of knowledge. It serves feeling. It serves to get from this place to that place. But if you don't honor those places, then the road is meaningless. Too often, that's what happens with the worship of rationality and that circular, academic, analytic thinking. But ultimately, I don't see feel/think as a dichotomy. I see them as a choice of ways and combinations.

Adrienne: Which we are constantly making. We don't make it once and for all. We constantly have to be making it, depending on where we are, over and over.

Audre: But I do think that we have been taught to think, to codify information in certain old ways, to learn, to understand in certain ways. The possible shapes of what has not been before exist only in that back place, where we keep those unnamed, untamed longings for something different and beyond what is now called possible, and to which our understanding can only build roads, But we have been taught to deny those fruitful areas of ourselves. I personally believe that the Black mother exists more in women; yet she is the name for a humanity that men are not without. But they have taken a position against that piece of themselves, and it is a world position, a position throughout time. And I've said this to you before, Adrienne, I feel that we're evolving. In terms of a species . . .

Adrienne: That women are evolving . . .

Audre: That the human race is evolving through women. That it's not by accident that there are more and more women — this sounds crazy, doesn't it — women being born, women surviving . . . and we've got to take that promise of new power seriously, or we'll make the same mistakes all over again. Unless we learn the lessons of the Black mother in each of us, whether we are Black or not . . . I believe this power exists in men also but they choose not to deal with it; which is, as I learned, their right. Hopefully this choice can be affected, but I don't know. I don't believe this shift from conquering problems to experiencing life is a one-generational shot or a single investment. I believe it's a whole signature which you try to set in motion and have some input into. But I'm not saying that women don't think or analyze. Or that white does not feel. I'm saying that we must never close our eyes to the terror, to the chaos which is Black which is creative which is female which is dark which is rejected which is messy which is . . .

Adrienne: Sinister . . .

Audre: Sinister, smelly, erotic, confused, upsetting . . .

Adrienne: I think we have to keep using and affirming a vocabulary that has been used negatively and perjoratively. And I assume that's the statement you're making in that sentence, that you make over and over in your poetry. And it's nothing as simplistic as saying "Black is beautiful," either.

Audre: There's nothing beautiful about a black machine. You know, Adrienne, when I was in high school, the editor of the school magazine said to me, softening her rejection of a poem, "After all, Audre, you don't want to be a sensualist poet."

Adrienne: I was told, as a poet, you're not supposed to be angry, you're not supposed to be personal.

Audre: After I published "Uses of the Erotic," a number of women who read it said that this is antifeminist, that the use of the erotic as a guide is . . .

Adrienne: Antifeminist?

Audre: Is reducing us once again to the unseen, the unusable. That in writing it I am returning us to a place of total intuition without insight.

Adrienne: And yet, in that essay you're talking about work and power, about two of the most political things that exist.

Audre: Yes, but what they see is . . . and I address this at the very beginning: I try to say that the erotic has been used against us, even the word itself, so often, that we have been taught to suspect what is deepest in ourselves, and that is the way we learn to testify against ourselves, against our feelings. When we talk in terms of our lives and our survival as women, we can use our knowledge of the erotic creatively. The way you get people to testify against themselves is not to have police tactics and oppressive techniques. What you do is to build it in so people learn to distrust everything in themselves that has not been sanctioned, to reject what is most creative in themselves to begin with, so you don't even need to stamp it out. A Black woman devaluating another Black woman's work. The Black women buying that hot comb and putting it in my locker at the library. It wasn't even Black men; it was Black women testifying against ourselves. This turning away from the erotic on the part of some of our best minds, our most creative and analytic women, is disturbing and destructive. Because we cannot fight old power in old power terms only. The only way we can do it is by creating another whole structure that touches every aspect of our existence, at the same time as we are resisting.

Adrienne: And as you were saying about courses, Black studies, women's studies: this is not just a question of being "allowed" to have our history or literature or theory in the old power framework. It is every minute of our lives, from our dreams to getting up and brushing our teeth to when we go to teach . . .

Audre: There are different choices facing Black and white women in life, certain specifically different pitfalls surrounding us because of our experiences, our color. Not only are some of the problems that face us dissimilar, but some of the entrapments and the weapons used to neutralize us are not the same.

Adrienne: I wish we could explore this more, about you and me, but also in general. I think it needs to be talked about, written about: the differences in alternatives or choices we are offered as Black and white women. There is a danger of seeing it in an all-or-nothing way. I think it is a very complex thing. White women are constantly offered choices or the appearance of choices. But also real choices that are undeniable. We don't always perceive the difference between the two.

Audre: Adrienne, in my journals I have a lot of pieces of conversations that I'm having with you in my head. I'll be having a conversation with you and I'll put it in my journal because stereotypically or symbolically these conversations occur in a space of Black woman/white woman where it's beyond Adrienne and Audre, almost as if we're two voices.

Adrienne: You mean the conversations you have in your head and your journal, or the conversations we're having on this earth?

Audre: The conversations that exist in my head that I put in the journal. This piece, I think, is one of them — about the different pitfalls. I've never forgotten the impatience in your voice that time on the telephone, when you said, "It's not enough to say to me that you intuit it." Do you remember? I will never forget that. Even at the same time that I understood what you meant, I felt a total wipeout of my modus, my way of perceiving and formulating.

Adrienne: Yes, but it's not a wipeout of your modus. Because I don't think my modus in unintuitive, right? And one of the crosses I've borne all my life is being told that I'm rational, logical, cool — I am not cool, and I'm not rational and logical in that icy sense. But there's a way in which, trying to translate from your experience to mine, I do need to hear chapter and verse from time to time. I'm afraid of it all slipping away into: "Ah, yes, I understand you." You remember, that telephone conversation was in connection with the essay I was writing on feminism and racism. I was trying to say to you, don't let's let this evolve into "You don't understand me" or "I can't understand you" or "Yes, of course we understand each other because we love each other." That's bullshit. So if I ask for documentation, it's because I take seriously the spaces between us that difference has created, that racism has created. There are times when I simply cannot assume that I know what you know, unless you show me what you mean.

Audre: But I'm used to associating a request for documentation as a questioning of my perceptions, an attempt to devalue what I'm in the process of discovering.

Adrienne: It's not. Help me to perceive what you perceive. That's what I'm trying to say to you.

Audre: But documentation does not help one perceive. At best it only analyzes the perception. At worst, it provides a screen by which to avoid concentrating on the core revelation, following it down to how it feels. Again, knowledge and understanding. They can function in concert, but they don't replace each other. But I'm not rejecting your need for documentation.

Adrienne: And in fact, I feel you've been giving it to me, in your poems always, and most recently in the long prose piece you've been writing,* and in talks we've been having. I don't feel the absence of it now.

---

* *Zami: A New Spelling of My Name*, originally published by Persephone Press in 1982 and reissued by Crossing Press in 1983.

Audre: Don't forget I'm a librarian. I became a librarian because I really believed I would gain tools for ordering and analyzing information. I couldn't know everything in the world, but I would gain tools for learning it. But that was of limited value. I can document the road to Abomey for you, and true, you might not get there without that information. I can respect what you're saying. But once you get there, only you know why, what you came for, as you search for it and perhaps find it.

So at certain stages that request for documentation is a blinder, a questioning of my perceptions. Someone once said to me that I hadn't documented the goddess in Africa, the woman bond that moves throughout *The Black Unicorn.** I had to laugh. I'm a poet, not a historian. I've shared my knowledge, I hope. Now you go document it, if you wish.

I don't know about you, Adrienne, but I have a difficult enough time making my perceptions verbal, tapping that deep place, forming that handle, and documentation at that point is often useless. Perceptions precede analysis just as visions precede action or accomplishments. It's like getting a poem . . .

That's the only thing I've had to fight with, my whole life, preserving my perceptions of how things are, and later, learning how to accept and correct at the same time. Doing this in the face of tremendous opposition and cruel judgment. And I spent a long time questioning my perceptions and my interior knowledge, not dealing with them, being tripped by them.

Adrienne: Well, I think that there's another element in all this between us. Certainly in that particular conversation on the telephone where I said you have to tell me chapter and verse. I've had great resistance to some of your perceptions. They can be very painful to me. Perceptions about what goes on between us, what goes on between Black and white people, what goes on between Black and white women. So, it's not that I can just accept your perceptions unblinkingly. Some of them are very hard for me. But I don't want to deny them. I know I can't afford to. I may have to take a long hard look and say, "Is this something I can use? What do I do with this?" I have to try to stand back and

* *The Black Unicorn* (W.W. Norton and Company, New York, 1978).

not become immersed in what you so forcefully are pronounc-ing. So there's a piece of me that wants to resist wholly, and a piece that wants to accept wholly, and there's some place in be-tween where I have to find my own ground. What I can't afford is either to wipe out your perceptions or to pretend I understand you when I don't. And then, if it's a question of racism — and I don't mean just the overt violence out there but also all the dif-ferences in our ways of seeing — there's always the question: "How do I use this? What do I do about it?"

Audre: "How much of this truth can I bear to see/ and still live/ unblinded?/ How much of this pain/ can I use?"* What holds us all back is being unable to ask that crucial question, that essential step deflected. You know the piece I wrote for *The Black Scholar?*** The piece was useful, but limited, because I didn't ask some essential question. And not having asked myself that question, not having realized that it was a question, I was deflecting a lot of energy in that piece. I kept reading it over, thinking, this isn't quite what it should be. I thought at the time I was holding back because it would be totally unacceptable in *The Black Scholar.* That wasn't it, really. I was holding back because I had not asked myself the question: "Why is women loving women so threatening to Black men unless they want to assume the white male position?" It was a question of how much I could bear, and of not realizing I could bear more than I thought I could at the time. It was also a question of how could I use that perception other than just in rage or destruction.

Adrienne: Speaking of rage and destruction, what do you real-ly mean by the first five lines of "Power"?***

Audre: "The difference between poetry/ and rhetoric/ is be-ing/ ready to kill yourself/ instead of your children." What was I feeling? I was very involved in a case . . .

Adrienne: The white policeman who shot the Black child and was acquitted. We had lunch around the time you were writing that poem and you were full of it.

---

* From "Need: A Choral of Black Women's Voices" in *Chosen Poems*, p. 115.
** "Scratching the Surface: Some Notes on Barriers to Women and Loving," see p. 45.
*** *The Black Unicorn*, pp. 108-110.

Audre: I was driving in the car and heard the news on the radio that the cop had been acquitted. I was really sickened with fury, and I decided to pull over and just jot some things down in my notebook to enable me to cross town without an accident because I felt so sick and so enraged. And I wrote those lines down — I was just writing, and that poem came out without craft. That's probably why I was talking to you about it because I didn't feel it was really a poem. I was thinking that the killer had been a student at John Jay and that I might have seen him in the hall, that I might see him again. What was retribution? What could have been done? There was one Black woman on the jury. It could have been me. Now I am here teaching in John Jay College. Do I kill him? What is my effective role? Would I kill her in the same way — the Black woman on the jury. What kind of strength did she, would I, have at the point of deciding to take a position . . .

Adrienne: Against eleven white men . . .

Audre: . . . that atavistic fear of an articulated power that is not on your terms. There is the jury — white male power, white male structures — how do you take a position against them? How do you reach down into threatening difference without being killed or killing? How do you deal with things you believe, live them not as theory, not even as emotion, but right on the line of action and effect and change? All of those things were riding in on that poem. But I had no sense, no understanding at the time, of the connections, just that I was that woman. And that to put myself on the line to do what had to be done at any place and time was so difficult, yet absolutely crucial, and not to do so was the most awful death. And putting yourself on the line is like killing a piece of yourself, in the sense that you have to kill, end, destroy something familiar and dependable, so that something new can come, in ourselves, in our world. And that sense of writing at the edge, out of urgency, not because you choose it but because you have to, that sense of survival — that's what the poem is out of, as well as the pain of my spiritual son's death over and over. Once you live any piece of your vision it opens you to a constant onslaught. Of necessities, of horrors, but of wonders too, of possibilities.

Adrienne: I was going to say, tell it on the other side.

Audre: Of wonders, absolute wonders, possibilities, like meteor showers all the time, bombardment, constant connections. And then, trying to separate what is useful for survival from what is distorted, destructive to self.

Adrienne: There's so much with which that has to be done — rejecting the distortions, keeping what we can use. Even in work created by people we admire intensely.

Audre: Yes, a commitment to being selectively open. I had to do that with my physical survival. How am I going to live with cancer and not succumb to it in the many ways that I could? What do I have to do? And coming up against, there's no one to tell you even possibilities. In the hospital I kept thinking, let's see, there's got to be someone somewhere, a Black lesbian feminist with cancer, how'd she handle it? Then I realized, hey, honey, you are it, for now. I read all of those books and then I realized, no one can tell me how to do it. I have to pick and choose, see what feels right. Determination, poetry — well that's all in the work.

Adrienne: I'm thinking about when you had just had the first biopsy, in 1977, and we were both supposed to speak on a panel in Chicago. On "The Transformation of Silence into Language and Action." And you said there was no way you were going to the MLA — remember? That you couldn't do it, you didn't need to do it, that doing it could not mean anything important to you. But in fact you went out there and said what you said, and it was for yourself but not only for yourself.

Audre: You said, "Why don't you tell them about what you've just been through?" And I started saying, "Now that doesn't have anything to do with the panel." And as I said that, I felt the words "Silence," "Transformation." I hadn't spoken about this experience. . . . This is silence. . . . Can I transform this? Is there any connection? Most of all, how do I share it? And that's how a setting down became clear on paper, as if the connections became clear in the setting down. That paper* and "A Litany for Survival"** came about at the same time. I had the feeling,

---

* See "The Transformation of Silence into Language and Action," see p. 40.
** *The Black Unicorn*, p. 31.

probably a body sense, that life was never going to be the same. If not now, eventually, this was something I would have to face. If not cancer, then somehow, I would have to examine the terms and means as well as the whys of my survival — and in the face of alteration. So much of the work I did, I did before I knew consciously that I had cancer. Questions of death and dying, dealing with power and strength, the sense of "What am I paying for?" that I wrote about in that paper, were crucial to me a year later. "Uses of the Erotic" was written four weeks before I found out I had breast cancer, in 1978.

Adrienne: Again, it's like what you were saying before, about making the poems that didn't exist, that you needed to have exist.

Audre: The existence of that paper enabled me to pick up and go to Houston and California; it enabled me to start working again. I don't know when I'd have been able to write again, if I hadn't had those words. Do you realize, we've come full circle, because that is where knowing and understanding mesh. What understanding begins to do is to make knowledge available for use, and that's the urgency, that's the push, that's the drive. I don't know how I wrote the long prose piece I have just finished, but I just knew that I had to do it.

Adrienne: That you had to understand what you knew and also make it available to others.

Audre: That's right. Inseparable process now. But for me, I had to know I knew it first — I had to feel.

The Master's Tools Will Never Dismantle the Master's House*

I AGREED TO TAKE PART in a New York University Institute for the Humanities conference a year ago, with the understanding that I would be commenting upon papers dealing with the role of difference within the lives of american women: difference of race, sexuality, class, and age. The absence of these considerations weakens any feminist discussion of the personal and the political.

It is a particular academic arrogance to assume any discussion of feminist theory without examining our many differences, and without a significant input from poor women, Black and Third World women, and lesbians. And yet, I stand here as a Black lesbian feminist, having been invited to comment within the only panel at this conference where the input of Black feminists and lesbians is represented. What this says about the vision of this conference is sad, in a country where racism, sexism, and homophobia are inseparable. To read this program is to assume that lesbian and Black women have nothing to say about existentialism, the erotic, women's culture and silence, developing feminist theory, or heterosexuality and power. And what does it mean in personal and political terms when even the two Black women who did present here were literally found at the last hour? What does it mean when the tools of a racist patriarchy

---

* Comments at "The Personal and the Political Panel," Second Sex Conference, New York, September 29, 1979.

are used to examine the fruits of that same patriarchy? It means that only the most narrow perimeters of change are possible and allowable.

The absence of any consideration of lesbian consciousness or the consciousness of Third World women leaves a serious gap within this conference and within the papers presented here. For example, in a paper on material relationships between women, I was conscious of an either/or model of nurturing which totally dismissed my knowledge as a Black lesbian. In this paper there was no examination of mutuality between women, no systems of shared support, no interdependence as exists between lesbians and women-identified women. Yet it is only in the patriarchal model of nurturance that women "who attempt to emancipate themselves pay perhaps too high a price for the results," as this paper states.

For women, the need and desire to nurture each other is not pathological but redemptive, and it is within that knowledge that our real power is rediscovered. It is this real connection which is so feared by a patriarchal world. Only within a patriarchal structure is maternity the only social power open to women.

Interdependency between women is the way to a freedom which allows the I to be, not in order to be used, but in order to be creative. This is a difference between the passive be and the active being.

Advocating the mere tolerance of difference between women is the grossest reformism. It is a total denial of the creative function of difference in our lives. Difference must be not merely tolerated, but seen as a fund of necessary polarities between which our creativity can spark like a dialectic. Only then does the necessity for interdependency become unthreatening. Only within that interdependency of different strengths, acknowledged and equal, can the power to seek new ways of being in the world generate, as well as the courage and sustenance to act where there are no charters.

Within the interdependence of mutual (nondominant) differences lies that security which enables us to descend into the chaos of knowledge and return with true visions of our future, along with the concomitant power to effect those changes which can bring that future into being. Difference is that raw and powerful connection from which our personal power is forged.

As women, we have been taught either to ignore our differences, or to view them as causes for separation and suspicion rather than as forces for change. Without community there is no liberation, only the most vulnerable and temporary armistice between an individual and her oppression. But community must not mean a shedding of our differences, nor the pathetic pretense that these differences do not exist.

Those of us who stand outside the circle of this society's definition of acceptable women; those of us who have been forged in the crucibles of difference — those of us who are poor, who are lesbians, who are Black, who are older — know that *survival is not an academic skill*. It is learning how to stand alone, unpopular and sometimes reviled, and how to make common cause with those others identified as outside the structures in order to define and seek a world in which we can all flourish. It is learning how to take our differences and make them strengths. *For the master's tools will never dismantle the master's house.* They may allow us temporarily to beat him at his own game, but they will never enable us to bring about genuine change. And this fact is only threatening to those women who still define the master's house as their only source of support.

Poor women and women of Color know there is a difference between the daily manifestations of marital slavery and prostitution because it is our daughters who line 42nd Street. If white american feminist theory need not deal with the differences between us, and the resulting difference in our oppressions, then how do you deal with the fact that the women who clean your houses and tend your children while you attend conferences on feminist theory are, for the most part, poor women and women of Color? What is the theory behind racist feminism?

In a world of possibility for us all, our personal visions help lay the groundwork for political action. The failure of academic feminists to recognize difference as a crucial strength is a failure to reach beyond the first patriarchal lesson. In our world, divide and conquer must become define and empower.

Why weren't other women of Color found to participate in this conference? Why were two phone calls to me considered a consultation? Am I the only possible source of names of Black feminists? And although the Black panelist's paper ends on an important and powerful connection of love between women, what about interracial cooperation between feminists who don't love each other?

In academic feminist circles, the answer to these questions is often, "We did not know who to ask." But that is the same evasion of responsibility, the same cop-out, that keeps Black women's art out of women's exhibitions, Black women's work out of most feminist publications except for the occasional "Special Third World Women's Issue," and Black women's texts off your reading lists. But as Adrienne Rich pointed out in a recent talk, white feminists have educated themselves about such an enormous amount over the past ten years, how come you haven't also educated yourselves about Black women and the differences between us — white and Black — when it is key to our survival as a movement?

Women of today are still being called upon to stretch across the gap of male ignorance and to educate men as to our existence and our needs. This is an old and primary tool of all oppressors to keep the oppressed occupied with the master's concerns. Now we hear that it is the task of women of Color to educate white women — in the face of tremendous resistance — as to our existence, our differences, our relative roles in our joint survival. This is a diversion of energies and a tragic repetition of racist patriarchal thought.

Simone de Beauvoir once said: "It is in the knowledge of the genuine conditions of our lives that we must draw our strength to live and our reasons for acting."

Racism and homophobia are real conditions of all our lives in this place and time. *I urge each one of us here to reach down into that deep place of knowledge inside herself and touch that terror and loathing of any difference that lives there. See whose face it wears.* Then the personal as the political can begin to illuminate all our choices.

Age, Race, Class, and Sex: Women Redefining Difference*

MUCH OF WESTERN EUROPEAN history conditions us to see human differences in simplistic opposition to each other: dominant/subordinate, good/bad, up/down, superior/inferior. In a society where the good is defined in terms of profit rather than in terms of human need, there must always be some group of people who, through systematized oppression, can be made to feel surplus, to occupy the place of the dehumanized inferior. Within this society, that group is made up of Black and Third World people, working-class people, older people, and women.

As a forty-nine-year-old Black lesbian feminist socialist mother of two, including one boy, and a member of an interracial couple, I usually find myself a part of some group defined as other, deviant, inferior, or just plain wrong. Traditionally, in american society, it is the members of oppressed, objectified groups who are expected to stretch out and bridge the gap between the actualities of our lives and the consciousness of our oppressor. For in order to survive, those of us for whom oppression is as american as apple pie have always had to be watchers, to become familiar with the language and manners of the oppressor, even sometimes adopting them for some illusion of protection. Whenever the need for some pretense of communication arises, those who profit from our oppression call upon us to share our knowledge with them. In other words, it is the responsibility of the oppressed to teach the oppressors their mistakes. I

---

* Paper delivered at the Copeland Colloquium, Amherst College, April 1980.

114

am responsible for educating teachers who dismiss my children's culture in school. Black and Third World people are expected to educate white people as to our humanity. Women are expected to educate men. Lesbians and gay men are expected to educate the heterosexual world. The oppressors maintain their position and evade responsibility for their own actions. There is a constant drain of energy which might be better used in redefining ourselves and devising realistic scenarios for altering the present and constructing the future.

Institutionalized rejection of difference is an absolute necessity in a profit economy which needs outsiders as surplus people. As members of such an economy, we have *all* been programmed to respond to the human differences between us with fear and loathing and to handle that difference in one of three ways: ignore it, and if that is not possible, copy it if we think it is dominant, or destroy it if we think it is subordinate. But we have no patterns for relating across our human differences as equals. As a result, those differences have been misnamed and misused in the service of separation and confusion.

Certainly there are very real differences between us of race, age, and sex. But it is not those differences between us that are separating us. It is rather our refusal to recognize those differences, and to examine the distortions which result from our misnaming them and their effects upon human behavior and expectation.

Racism, the belief in the inherent superiority of one race over all others and thereby the right to dominance. Sexism, the belief in the inherent superiority of one sex over the other and thereby the right to dominance. Ageism. Heterosexism. Elitism. Classism.

It is a lifetime pursuit for each one of us to extract these distortions from our living at the same time as we recognize, reclaim, and define those differences upon which they are imposed. For we have all been raised in a society where those distortions were endemic within our living. Too often, we pour the energy needed for recognizing and exploring difference into pretending those differences are insurmountable barriers, or that they do not exist at all. This results in a voluntary isolation, or false and treacherous connections. Either way, we do not develop tools for using human difference as a springboard for creative change within our lives. We speak not of human difference, but of human deviance.

Somewhere, on the edge of consciousness, there is what I call a *mythical norm*, which each one of us within our hearts knows "that is not me." In america, this norm is usually defined as white, thin, male, young, heterosexual, christian, and financially secure. It is with this mythical norm that the trappings of power reside within this society. Those of us who stand outside that power often identify one way in which we are different, and we assume that to be the primary cause of all oppression, forgetting other distortions around difference, some of which we ourselves may be practising. By and large within the women's movement today, white women focus upon their oppression as women and ignore differences of race, sexual preference, class, and age. There is a pretense to a homogeneity of experience covered by the word *sisterhood* that does not in fact exist.

Unacknowledged class differences rob women of each others' energy and creative insight. Recently a women's magazine collective made the decision for one issue to print only prose, saying poetry was a less "rigorous" or "serious" art form. Yet even the form our creativity takes is often a class issue. Of all the art forms, poetry is the most economical. It is the one which is the most secret, which requires the least physical labor, the least material, and the one which can be done between shifts, in the hospital pantry, on the subway, and on scraps of surplus paper. Over the last few years, writing a novel on tight finances, I came to appreciate the enormous differences in the material demands between poetry and prose. As we reclaim our literature, poetry has been the major voice of poor, working class, and Colored women. A room of one's own may be a necessity for writing prose, but so are reams of paper, a typewriter, and plenty of time. The actual requirements to produce the visual arts also help determine, along class lines, whose art is whose. In this day of inflated prices for material, who are our sculptors, our painters, our photographers? When we speak of a broadly based women's culture, we need to be aware of the effect of class and economic differences on the supplies available for producing art.

As we move toward creating a society within which we can each flourish, ageism is another distortion of relationship which interferes without vision. By ignoring the past, we are encouraged to repeat its mistakes. The "generation gap" is an important social tool for any repressive society. If the younger members of a community view the older members as contemptible or suspect or excess, they will never be able to join hands and examine the living memories of the community, nor ask the all important question, "Why?" This gives rise to a historical amnesia that keeps us working to invent the wheel every time we have to go to the store for bread.

We find ourselves having to repeat and relearn the same old lessons over and over that our mothers did because we do not pass on what we have learned, or because we are unable to listen. For instance, how many times has this all been said before? For another, who would have believed that once again our daughters are allowing their bodies to be hampered and purgatoried by girdles and high heels and hobble skirts?

Ignoring the differences of race between women and the implications of those differences presents the most serious threat to the mobilization of women's joint power.

As white women ignore their built-in privilege of whiteness and define *woman* in terms of their own experience alone, then women of Color become "other," the outsider whose experience and tradition is too "alien" to comprehend. An example of this is the signal absence of the experience of women of Color as a resource for women's studies courses. The literature of women of Color is seldom included in women's literature courses and almost never in other literature courses, nor in women's studies as a whole. All too often, the excuse given is that the literatures of women of Color can only be taught by Colored women, or that they are too difficult to understand, or that classes cannot "get into" them because they come out of experiences that are "too different." I have heard this argument presented by white women of otherwise quite clear intelligence, women who seem to have no trouble at all teaching and reviewing work that comes out of the vastly different experiences of Shakespeare, Molière, Dostoyefsky, and Aristophanes. Surely there must be some other explanation.

This is a very complex question, but I believe one of the reasons white women have such difficulty reading Black women's work is because of their reluctance to see Black women as women and different from themselves. To examine Black women's literature effectively requires that we be seen as whole people in our actual complexities — as individuals, as women, as human — rather than as one of those problematic but familiar stereotypes provided in this society in place of genunine images of Black women. And I believe this holds true for the literatures of other women of Color who are not Black.

The literatures of all women of Color recreate the textures of our lives, and many white women are heavily invested in ignoring the real differences. For as long as any difference between us means one of us must be inferior, then the recognition of any difference must be fraught with guilt. To allow women of Color to step out of stereotypes is too guilt provoking, for it threatens the complacency of those women who view oppression only in terms of sex.

Refusing to recognize difference makes it impossible to see the different problems and pitfalls facing us as women.

Thus, in a patriarchal power system where whiteskin privilege is a major prop, the entrapments used to neutralize Black women and white women are not the same. For example, it is easy for Black women to be used by the power structure against Black men, not because they are men, but because they are Black. Therefore, for Black women, it is necessary at all times to separate the needs of the oppressor from our own legitimate conflicts within our communities. This same problem does not exist for white women. Black women and men have shared racist oppression and still share it, although in different ways. Out of that shared oppression we have developed joint defenses and joint vulnerabilities to each other that are not duplicated in the white community, with the exception of the relationship between Jewish women and Jewish men.

On the other hand, white women face the pitfall of being seduced into joining the oppressor under the pretense of sharing power. This possibility does not exist in the same way for women of Color. The tokenism that is sometimes extended to us is not an invitation to join power; our racial "otherness" is a visible reality that makes that quite clear. For white women

there is a wider range of pretended choices and rewards for identifying with patriarchal power and its tools.

Today, with the defeat of ERA, the tightening economy, and
increased conservatism, it is easier once again for white women
to believe the dangerous fantasy that if you are good enough,
pretty enough, sweet enough, quiet enough, teach the children
to behave, hate the right people, and marry the right men, then
you will be allowed to co-exist with patriarchy in relative peace,
at least until a man needs your job or the neighborhood rapist
happens along. And true, unless one lives and loves in the
trenches it is difficult to remember that the war against dehumanization is ceaseless.

But Black women and our children know the fabric of our
lives is stitched with violence and with hatred, that there is no
rest. We do not deal with it only on the picket lines, or in dark
midnight alleys, or in the places where we dare to verbalize our
resistance. For us, increasingly, violence weaves through the
daily tissues of our living — in the supermarket, in the
classroom, in the elevator, in the clinic and the schoolyard,
from the plumber, the baker, the saleswoman, the bus driver,
the bank teller, the waitress who does not serve us.

Some problems we share as women, some we do not. You fear
your children will grow up to join the patriarchy and testify
against you, we fear our children will be dragged from a car and
shot down in the street, and you will turn your backs upon the
reasons they are dying.

The threat of difference has been no less blinding to people of
Color. Those of us who are Black must see that the reality of
our lives and our struggle does not make us immune to the errors of ignoring and misnaming difference. Within Black communities where racism is a living reality, differences among us
often seem dangerous and suspect. The need for unity is often
misnamed as a need for homogeneity, and a Black feminist vision mistaken for betrayal of our common interests as a people.
Because of the continuous battle against racial erasure that
Black women and Black men share, some Black women still
refuse to recognize that we are also oppressed as women, and
that sexual hostility against Black women is practiced not only

by the white racist society, but implemented within our Black communities as well. It is a disease striking the heart of Black nationhood, and silence will not make it disappear. Exacerbated by racism and the pressures of powerlessness, violence against Black women and children often becomes a standard within our communities, one by which manliness can be measured. But these woman-hating acts are rarely discussed as crimes against Black women.

As a group, women of Color are the lowest paid wage earners in america. We are the primary targets of abortion and steriliza-tion abuse, here and abroad. In certain parts of Africa, small girls are still being sewed shut between their legs to keep them docile and for men's pleasure. This is known as female circumci-sion, and it is not a cultural affair as the late Jomo Kenyatta in-sisted, it is a crime against Black women.

Black women's literature is full of the pain of frequent assault, not only by a racist patriarchy, but also by Black men. Yet the necessity for and history of shared battle have made us, Black women, particularly vulnerable to the false accusation that anti-sexist is anti-Black. Meanwhile, womanhating as a recourse of the powerless is sapping strength from Black communities, and our very lives. Rape is on the increase, reported and unreported, and rape is not aggressive sexuality, it is sexualized aggression. As Kalamu ya Salaam, a Black male writer points out, "As long as male domination exists, rape will exist. Only women revolting and men made conscious of their responsibility to fight sexism can collectively stop rape."*

Differences between ourselves as Black women are also being misnamed and used to separate us from one another. As a Black lesbian feminist comfortable with the many different ingre-dients of my identity, and a woman committed to racial and sexual freedom from oppression, I find I am constantly being en-couraged to pluck out some one aspect of myself and present this as the meaningful whole, eclipsing or denying the other parts of self. But this is a destructive and fragmenting way to live. My fullest concentration of energy is available to me only when I integrate all the parts of who I am, openly, allowing

* From "Rape: A Radical Analysis, An African-American Perspective" by Kalamu ya Salaam in *Black Books Bulletin*, vol. 6, no. 4 (1980).

power from particular sources of my living to flow back and forth freely through all my different selves, without the restrictions of externally imposed definition. Only then can I bring myself and my energies as a whole to the service of those struggles which I embrace as part of my living.

A fear of lesbians, or of being accused of being a lesbian, has led many Black women into testifying against themselves. It has led some of us into destructive alliances, and others into despair and isolation. In the white women's communities, heterosexism is sometimes a result of identifying with the white patriarchy, a rejection of that interdependence between women-identified women which allows the self to be, rather than to be used in the service of men. Sometimes it reflects a die-hard belief in the protective coloration of heterosexual relationships, sometimes a self-hate which all women have to fight against, taught us from birth.

Although elements of these attitudes exist for all women, there are particular resonances of heterosexism and homophobia among Black women. Despite the fact that woman-bonding has a long and honorable history in the African and Africanamerican communities, and despite the knowledge and accomplishments of many strong and creative women-identified Black women in the political, social and cultural fields, heterosexual Black women often tend to ignore or discount the existence and work of Black lesbians. Part of this attitude has come from an understandable terror of Black male attack within the close confines of Black society, where the punishment for any female self-assertion is still to be accused of being a lesbian and therefore unworthy of the attention or support of the scarce Black male. But part of this need to misname and ignore Black lesbians comes from a very real fear that openly women-identified Black women who are no longer dependent upon men for their self-definition may well reorder our whole concept of social relationships.

Black women who once insisted that lesbianism was a white woman's problem now insist that Black lesbians are a threat to Black nationhood, are consorting with the enemy, are basically un-Black. These accusations, coming from the very women to whom we look for deep and real understanding, have served to keep many Black lesbians in hiding, caught between the racism of white women and the homophobia of their sisters. Often, their work has been ignored, trivialized, or misnamed, as with the work of Angelina Grimke, Alice Dunbar-Nelson, Lorraine Hansberry. Yet women-bonded women have always been some part of the power of Black communities, from our unmarried aunts to the amazons of Dahomey.

And it is certainly not Black lesbians who are assaulting women and raping children and grandmothers on the streets of our communities.

Across this country, as in Boston during the spring of 1979 following the unsolved murders of twelve Black women, Black lesbians are spearheading movements against violence against Black women.

What are the particular details within each of our lives that can be scrutinized and altered to help bring about change? How do we redefine difference for all women? It is not our differences which separate women, but our reluctance to recognize those differences and to deal effectively with the distortions which have resulted from the ignoring and misnaming of those differences.

As a tool of social control, women have been encouraged to recognize only one area of human difference as legitimate, those differences which exist between women and men. And we have learned to deal across those differences with the urgency of all oppressed subordinates. All of us have had to learn to live or work or coexist with men, from our fathers on. We have recognized and negotiated these differences, even when this recognition only continued the old dominant/subordinate mode of human relationship, where the oppressed must recognize the masters' difference in order to survive.

But our future survival is predicated upon our ability to relate within equality. As women, we must root out internalized patterns of oppression within ourselves if we are to move beyond the most superficial aspects of social change. Now we must recognize differences among women who are our equals, neither inferior nor superior, and devise ways to use each others' difference to enrich our visions and our joint struggles.

The future of our earth may depend upon the ability of all women to identify and develop new definitions of power and new patterns of relating across difference. The old definitions have not served us, nor the earth that supports us. The old patterns, no matter how cleverly rearranged to imitate progress, still condemn us to cosmetically altered repetitions of the same old exchanges, the same old guilt, hatred, recrimination, lamentation, and suspicion.

For we have, built into all of us, old blueprints of expectation and response, old structures of oppression, and these must be altered at the same time as we alter the living conditions which are a result of those structures. For the master's tools will never dismantle the master's house.

As Paulo Freire shows so well in *The Pedagogy of the Oppressed*,* the true focus of revolutionary change is never merely the oppressive situations which we seek to escape, but that piece of the oppressor which is planted deep within each of us, and which knows only the oppressors' tactics, the oppressors' relationships.

Change means growth, and growth can be painful. But we sharpen self-definition by exposing the self in work and struggle together with those whom we define as different from ourselves, although sharing the same goals. For Black and white, old and young, lesbian and heterosexual women alike, this can mean new paths to our survival.

> *We have chosen each other*
> *and the edge of each others battles*
> *the war is the same*
> *if we lose*
> *someday women's blood will congeal*
> *upon a dead planet*
> *if we win*
> *there is no telling*
> *we seek beyond history*
> *for a new and more possible meeting.***

---

* Seabury Press, New York, 1970.

** From "Outlines," unpublished poem.

The Uses of Anger: Women Responding to Racism*

Racism. The belief in the inherent superiority of one race over all others and thereby the right to dominance, manifest and implied.

Women respond to racism. My response to racism is anger. I have lived with that anger, ignoring it, feeding upon it, learning to use it before it laid my visions to waste, for most of my life. Once I did it in silence, afraid of the weight. My fear of anger taught me nothing. Your fear of that anger will teach you nothing, also.

Women responding to racism means women responding to anger; the anger of exclusion, of unquestioned privilege, of racial distortions, of silence, ill-use, stereotyping, defensiveness, misnaming, betrayal, and co-optation.

My anger is a response to racist attitudes and to the actions and presumptions that arise out of those attitudes. If your dealings with other women reflect those attitudes, then my anger and your attendant fears are spotlights that can be used for growth in the same way I have used learning to express anger for my growth. But for corrective surgery, not guilt. Guilt and defensiveness are bricks in a wall against which we all flounder; they serve none of our futures.

Because I do not want this to become a theoretical discussion, I am going to give a few examples of interchanges between

---

* Keynote presentation at the National Women's Studies Association Conference, Storrs, Connecticut, June 1981.

women that illustrate these points. In the interest of time, I am going to cut them short. I want you to know there were many more.

For example:

• I speak out of direct and particular anger at an academic conference, and a white woman says, "Tell me how you feel but don't say it too harshly or I cannot hear you." But is it my manner that keeps her from hearing, or the threat of a message that her life may change?

• The Women's Studies Program of a southern university invites a Black woman to read following a week-long forum on Black and white women. "What has this week given to you?" I ask. The most vocal white woman says, "I think I've gotten a lot. I feel Black women really understand me a lot better now; they have a better idea of where I'm coming from." As if understanding her lay at the core of the racist problem.

• After fifteen years of a women's movement which professes to address the life concerns and possible futures of all women, I still hear, on campus after campus, "How can we address the issues of racism? No women of Color attended." Or, the other side of that statement, "We have no one in our department equipped to teach their work." In other words, racism is a Black women's problem, a problem of women of Color, and only we can discuss it.

• After I read from my work entitled "Poems for Women in Rage,"* a white woman asks me: "Are you going to do anything with how we can deal directly with *our* anger? I feel it's so important." I ask, "How do you use *your* rage?" And then I have to turn away from the blank look in her eyes, before she can invite me to participate in her own annihilation. I do not exist to feel her anger for her.

• White women are beginning to examine their relationships to Black women, yet often I hear them wanting only to deal with little colored children across the roads of childhood, the beloved nursemaid, the occasional second-grade classmate — those tender memories of what was once mysterious and intri-

---

* One poem from this series is included in *Chosen Poems: Old and New* (W.W. Norton and Company, New York, 1978), pp. 105-108.

guing or neutral. You avoid the childhood assumptions formed by the raucous laughter at Rastus and Alfalfa, the acute message of your mommy's handerkerchief spread upon the park bench because I had just been sitting there, the indelible and dehumanizing portraits of Amos 'n Andy and your daddy's humorous bedtime stories.

• I wheel my two-year-old daughter in a shopping cart through a supermarket in Eastchester in 1967, and a little white girl riding past in her mother's cart calls out excitedly, "Oh look, Mommy, a baby maid!" And your mother shushes you, but she does not correct you. And so fifteen years later, at a conference on racism, you can still find that story humorous. But I hear your laughter is full of terror and dis-ease.

• A white academic welcomes the appearance of a collection by non-Black women of Color.* "It allows me to deal with racism without dealing with the harshness of Black women," she says to me.

• At an international cultural gathering of women, a well-known white american woman poet interrupts the reading of the work of women of Color to read her own poem, and then dashes off to an "important panel."

If women in the academy truly want a dialogue about racism, it will require recognizing the needs and the living contexts of other women. When an academic woman says, "I can't afford it," she may mean she is making a choice about how to spend her available money. But when a woman on welfare says, "I can't afford it," she means she is surviving on an amount of money that was barely subsistence in 1972, and she often does not have enough to eat. Yet the National Women's Studies Association here in 1981 holds a conference in which it commits itself to responding to racism, yet refuses to waive the registration fee for poor women and women of Color who wished to present and conduct workshops. This has made it impossible for many women of Color — for instance, Wilmette Brown, of Black Women for Wages for Housework — to par-

---

* *This Bridge Called My Back: Writings by Radical Women of Color* edited by Cherríe Moraga and Gloria Anzaldua (Kitchen Table: Women of Color Press, New York, 1984), first published in 1981.

ticipate in this conference. Is this to be merely another case of the academy discussing life within the closed circuits of the academy?

To the white women present who recognize these attitudes as familiar, but most of all, to all my sisters of Color who live and survive thousands of such encounters — to my sisters of Color who like me still tremble their rage under harness, or who sometimes question the expression of our rage as useless and disruptive (the two most popular accusations) — I want to speak about anger, my anger, and what I have learned from my travels through its dominions.

Everything can be used / except what is wasteful / (you will need / to remember this when you are accused of destruction.)*

Every woman has a well-stocked arsenal of anger potentially useful against those oppressions, personal and institutional, which brought that anger into being. Focused with precision it can become a powerful source of energy serving progress and change. And when I speak of change, I do not mean a simple switch of positions or a temporary lessening of tensions, nor the ability to smile or feel good. I am speaking of a basic and radical alteration in those assumptions underlining our lives.

I have seen situations where white women hear a racist remark, resent what has been said, become filled with fury, and remain silent because they are afraid. That unexpressed anger lies within them like an undetonated device, usually to be hurled at the first woman of Color who talks about racism.

But anger expressed and translated into action in the service of our vision and our future is a liberating and strengthening act of clarification, for it is in the painful process of this translation that we identify who are our allies with whom we have grave differences, and who are our genuine enemies.

Anger is loaded with information and energy. When I speak of women of Color, I do not only mean Black women. The woman of Color who is not Black and who charges me with rendering her invisible by assuming that her struggles with

---

* From "For Each of You," first published in *From A Land Where Other People Live* (Broadside Press, Detroit, 1973), and collected in *Chosen Poems: Old and New* (W.W. Norton and Company, New York, 1982), p. 42.

racism are identical with my own has something to tell me that I had better learn from, lest we both waste ourselves fighting the truths between us. If I participate, knowingly or otherwise, in my sister's oppression and she calls me on it, to answer her anger with my own only blankets the substance of our exchange with reaction. It wastes energy. And yes, it is very difficult to stand still and to listen to another woman's voice delineate an agony I do not share, or one to which I myself have contributed.

In this place we speak removed from the more blatant reminders of our embattlement as women. This need not blind us to the size and complexities of the forces mounting against us and all that is most human within our environment. We are not here as women examining racism in a political and social vacuum. We operate in the teeth of a system for which racism and sexism are primary, established, and necessary props of profit. Women responding to racism is a topic so dangerous that when the local media attempt to discredit this conference they choose to focus upon the provision of lesbian housing as a diversionary device — as if the Hartford *Courant* dare not mention the topic chosen for discussion here, racism, lest it become apparent that women are in fact attempting to examine and to alter all the repressive conditions of our lives.

Mainstream communication does not want women, particularly white women, responding to racism. It wants racism to be accepted as an immutable given in the fabric of your existence, like eveningtime or the common cold.

So we are working in a context of opposition and threat, the cause of which is certainly not the angers which lie between us, but rather that virulent hatred leveled against all women, people of Color, lesbians and gay men, poor people — against all of us who are seeking to examine the particulars of our lives as we resist our oppressions, moving toward coalition and effective action.

Any discussion among women about racism must include the recognition and the use of anger. This discussion must be direct and creative because it is crucial. We cannot allow our fear of anger to deflect us nor seduce us into settling for anything less than the hard work of excavating honesty; we must be quite serious about the choice of this topic and the angers entwined within it because, rest assured, our opponents are quite serious about their hatred of us and of what we are trying to do here.

And while we scrutinize the often painful face of each other's anger, please remember that it is not our anger which makes me caution you to lock your doors at night and not to wander the streets of Hartford alone. It is the hatred which lurks in those streets, that urge to destroy us all if we truly work for change rather than merely indulge in academic rhetoric.

This hatred and our anger are very different. Hatred is the fury of those who do not share our goals, and its object is death and destruction. Anger is a grief of distortions between peers, and its object is change. But our time is getting shorter. We have been raised to view any difference other than sex as a reason for destruction, and for Black women and white women to face each other's angers without denial or immobility or silence or guilt is in itself a heretical and generative idea. It implies peers meeting upon a common basis to examine difference, and to alter those distortions which history has created around our difference. For it is those distortions which separate us. And we must ask ourselves: Who profits from all this?

Women of Color in america have grown up within a symphony of anger, at being silenced, at being unchosen, at knowing that when we survive, it is in spite of a world that takes for granted our lack of humanness, and which hates our very existence outside of its service. And I say *symphony* rather than *cacophony* because we have had to learn to orchestrate those furies so that they do not tear us apart. We have had to learn to move through them and use them for strength and force and insight within our daily lives. Those of us who did not learn this difficult lesson did not survive. And part of my anger is always libation for my fallen sisters.

Anger is an appropriate reaction to racist attitudes, as is fury when the actions arising from those attitudes do not change. To those women here who fear the anger of women of Color more than their own unscrutinized racist attitudes, I ask: Is the anger of women of Color more threatening than the woman-hatred that tinges all aspects of our lives?

It is not the anger of other women that will destroy us but our refusals to stand still, to listen to its rhythms, to learn within it, to move beyond the manner of presentation to the substance, to tap that anger as an important source of empowerment.

I cannot hide my anger to spare you guilt, nor hurt feelings, nor answering anger; for to do so insults and trivializes all our efforts. Guilt is not a response to anger; it is a response to one's own actions or lack of action. If it leads to change then it can be useful, since it is then no longer guilt but the beginning of knowledge. Yet all too often, guilt is just another name for impotence, for defensiveness destructive of communication; it becomes a device to protect ignorance and the continuation of things the way they are, the ultimate protection for changelessness.

Most women have not developed tools for facing anger constructively. CR groups in the past, largely white, dealt with how to express anger, usually at the world of men. And these groups were made up of white women who shared the terms of their oppressions. There was usually little attempt to articulate the genuine differences between women, such as those of race, color, age, class, and sexual identity. There was no apparent need at that time to examine the contradictions of self, woman as oppressor. There was work on expressing anger, but very little on anger directed against each other. No tools were developed to deal with other women's anger except to avoid it, deflect it, or flee from it under a blanket of guilt.

I have no creative use for guilt, yours or my own. Guilt is only another way of avoiding informed action, of buying time out of the pressing need to make clear choices, out of the approaching storm that can feed the earth as well as bend the trees. If I speak to you in anger, at least I have spoken to you: I have not put a gun to your head and shot you down in the street; I have not looked at your bleeding sister's body and asked, "What did she do to deserve it?" This was the reaction of two white women to Mary Church Terrell's telling of the lynching of a pregnant Black woman whose baby was then torn from her body. That was in 1921, and Alice Paul had just refused to publicly endorse the enforcement of the Nineteenth Amendment for all women

— by refusing to endorse the inclusion of women of Color, although we had worked to help bring about that amendment.

The angers between women will not kill us if we can articulate them with precision, if we listen to the content of what is said with at least as much intensity as we defend ourselves against the manner of saying. When we turn from anger we turn from insight, saying we will accept only the designs already known, deadly and safely familiar. I have tried to learn my anger's usefulness to me, as well as its limitations.

For women raised to fear, too often anger threatens annihilation. In the male construct of brute force, we were taught that our lives depended upon the good will of patriarchal power. The anger of others was to be avoided at all costs because there was nothing to be learned from it but pain, a judgment that we had been bad girls, come up lacking, not done what we were supposed to do. And if we accept our powerlessness, then of course any anger can destroy us.

But the strength of women lies in recognizing differences between us as creative, and in standing to those distortions which we inherited without blame, but which are now ours to alter. The angers of women can transform difference through insight into power. For anger between peers births change, not destruction, and the discomfort and sense of loss it often causes is not fatal, but a sign of growth.

My response to racism is anger. That anger has eaten clefts into my living only when it remained unspoken, useless to anyone. It has also served me in classrooms without light or learning, where the work and history of Black women was less than a vapor. It has served me as fire in the ice zone of uncomprehending eyes of white women who see in my experience and the experience of my people only new reasons for fear or guilt. And my anger is no excuse for not dealing with your blindness, no reason to withdraw from the results of your own actions.

When women of Color speak out of the anger that laces so many of our contacts with white women, we are often told that we are "creating a mood of hopelessness," "preventing white women from getting past guilt," or "standing in the way of trusting communication and action." All these quotes come directly from letters to me from members of this organization within the last two years. One woman wrote, "Because you are Black and Lesbian, you seem to speak with the moral authority of suffering." Yes, I am Black and Lesbian, and what you hear in my voice is fury, not suffering. Anger, not moral authority. There is a difference.

To turn aside from the anger of Black women with excuses or the pretexts of intimidation is to award no one power — it is merely another way of preserving racial blindness, the power of unaddressed privilege, unbreached, intact. Guilt is only another form of objectification. Oppressed peoples are always being asked to stretch a little more, to bridge the gap between blind-ness and humanity. Black women are expected to use our anger only in the service of other people's salvation or learning. But that time is over. My anger has meant pain to me but it has also meant survival, and before I give it up I'm going to be sure that there is something at least as powerful to replace it on the road to clarity.

What woman here is so enamoured of her own oppression that she cannot see her heelprint upon another woman's face? What woman's terms of oppression have become precious and necessary to her as a ticket into the fold of the righteous, away from the cold winds of self-scrutiny?

I am a lesbian woman of Color whose children eat regularly because I work in a university. If their full bellies make me fail to recognize my commonality with a woman of Color whose children do not eat because she cannot find work, or who has no children because her insides are rotted from home abortions and sterilization; if I fail to recognize the lesbian who chooses not to have children, the woman who remains closeted because her homophobic community is her only life support, the woman who chooses silence instead of another death, the woman who is terrified lest my anger trigger the explosion of hers; if I fail to recognize them as other faces of myself, then I am contributing not only to each of their oppressions but also to my own, and the anger which stands between us then must be used for clarity and mutual empowerment, not for evasion by guilt or for fur-ther separation. I am not free while any woman is unfree, even when her shackles are very different from my own. And I am not free as long as one person of Color remains chained. Nor is any one of you.

I speak here as a woman of Color who is not bent upon destruction, but upon survival. No woman is responsible for altering the psyche of her oppressor, even when that psyche is embodied in another woman. I have suckled the wolf's lip of anger and I have used it for illumination, laughter, protection, fire in places where there was no light, no food, no sisters, no quarter. We are not goddesses or matriarchs or edifices of divine forgiveness; we are not fiery fingers of judgment or instruments of flagellation; we are women forced back always upon our woman's power. We have learned to use anger as we have learned to use the dead flesh of animals, and bruised, battered, and changing, we have survived and grown and, in Angela Wilson's words, we *are* moving on. With or without uncolored women. We use whatever strengths we have fought for, including anger, to help define and fashion a world where all our sisters can grow, where our children can love, and where the power of touching and meeting another woman's difference and wonder will eventually transcend the need for destruction.

For it is not the anger of Black women which is dripping down over this globe like a diseased liquid. It is not my anger that launches rockets, spends over sixty thousand dollars a second on missiles and other agents of war and death, slaughters children in cities, stockpiles nerve gas and chemical bombs, sodomizes our daughters and our earth. It is not the anger of Black women which corrodes into blind, dehumanizing power, bent upon the annihilation of us all unless we meet it with what we have, our power to examine and to redefine the terms upon which we will live and work; our power to envision and to reconstruct, anger by painful anger, stone upon heavy stone, a future of pollinating difference and the earth to support our choices.

We welcome all women who can meet us, face to face, beyond objectification and beyond guilt.

Learning from the 60s*

MALCOLM X IS a distinct shape in a very pivotal period of my life. I stand here now — Black, Lesbian, Feminist — an inheritor of Malcolm and in his tradition, doing my work, and the ghost of his voice through my mouth asks each one of you here tonight: Are you doing yours?

There are no new ideas, just new ways of giving those ideas we cherish breath and power in our own living. I'm not going to pretend that the moment I first saw or heard Malcolm X he became my shining prince, because it wouldn't be true. In February 1965 I was raising two children and a husband in a three-room flat on 149th Street in Harlem. I had read about Malcolm X and the Black Muslims. I became more interested in Malcolm X after he left the Nation of Islam, when he was silenced by Elijah Muhammad for his comment, after Kennedy's assassination, to the effect that the chickens had come home to roost. Before this I had not given much thought to the Nation of Islam because of their attitude toward women as well as because of their nonactivist stance. I'd read Malcolm's autobiography, and I liked his style, and I thought he looked a lot like my father's people, but I was one of the ones who didn't really hear Malcolm's voice until it was amplified by death.

I had been guilty of what many of us are still guilty of — letting the media, and I don't mean only the white media — define the bearers of those messages most important to our lives.

When I read Malcolm X with careful attention, I found a man much closer to the complexities of real change than anything I

* Talk delivered at the Malcolm X Weekend, Harvard University, February 1982.

had read before. Much of what I say here tonight was born from his words.

In the last year of his life, Malcolm X added a breadth to his essential vision that would have brought him, had he lived, into inevitable confrontation with the question of difference as a creative and necessary force for change. For as Malcolm X progressed from a position of resistance to, and analysis of, the racial status quo, to more active considerations of organizing for change, he began to reassess some of his earlier positions. One of the most basic Black survival skills is the ability to change, to metabolize experience, good or ill, into something that is useful, lasting, effective. Four hundred years of survival as an endangered species has taught most of us that if we intend to live, we had better become fast learners. Malcolm knew this. We do not have to live the same mistakes over again if we can look at them, learn from them, and build upon them.

Before he was killed, Malcolm had altered and broadened his opinions concerning the role of women in society and the revolution. He was beginning to speak with increasing respect of the connection between himself and Martin Luther King, Jr., whose policies of nonviolence appeared to be so opposite to his own. And he began to examine the societal conditions under which alliances and coalitions must indeed occur.

He had also begun to discuss those scars of oppression which lead us to war against ourselves in each other rather than against our enemies.

As Black people, if there is one thing we can learn from the 60s, it is how infinitely complex any move for liberation must be. For we must move against not only those forces which dehumanize us from the outside, but also against those oppressive values which we have been forced to take into ourselves. Through examining the combination of our triumphs and errors, we can examine the dangers of an incomplete vision. Not to condemn that vision but to alter it, construct templates for possible futures, and focus our rage for change upon our enemies rather than upon each other. In the 1960s, the awakened anger of the Black community was often expressed, not vertically against the corruption of power and true sources of control over our lives, but horizontally toward those closest to us who mirrored our own impotence.

We were poised for attack, not always in the most effective places. When we disagreed with one another about the solution to a particular problem, we were often far more vicious to each other than to the originators of our common problem. Historically, difference had been used so cruelly against us that as a people we were reluctant to tolerate any diversion from what was externally defined as Blackness. In the 60s, political correctness became not a guideline for living, but a new set of shackles. A small and vocal part of the Black community lost sight of the fact that unity does not mean unanimity — Black people are not some standardly digestible quantity. In order to work together we do not have to become a mix of indistinguishable particles resembling a vat of homogenized chocolate milk. Unity implies the coming together of elements which are, to begin with, varied and diverse in their particular natures. Our persistence in examining the tensions within diversity encourages growth toward our common goal. So often we either ignore the past or romanticize it, render the reason for unity useless or mythic. We forget that the necessary ingredient needed to make the past work for the future is our energy in the present, metabolizing one into the other. Continuity does not happen automatically, nor is it a passive process.

The 60s were characterized by a heady belief in instantaneous solutions. They were vital years of awakening, of pride, and of error. The civil rights and Black power movements rekindled possibilities for disenfranchised groups within this nation. Even though we fought common enemies, at times the lure of individual solutions made us careless of each other. Sometimes we could not bear the face of each other's differences because of what we feared those differences might say about ourselves. As if everybody can't eventually be too Black, too white, too man, too woman. But any future vision which can encompass all of us, by definition, must be complex and expanding, not easy to achieve. The answer to cold is heat, the answer to hunger is food. But there is no simple monolithic solution to racism, to sexism, to homophobia. There is only the conscious focusing within each of my days to move against them, wherever I come up against these particular manifestations of the same disease. By seeing who the *we* is, we learn to use our energies with greater precision against our enemies rather than against ourselves.

In the 60s, white america — racist and liberal alike — was more than pleased to sit back as spectator while Black militant fought Black Muslim, Black Nationalist badmouthed the non-violent, and Black women were told that our only useful position in the Black Power movement was prone. The existence of Black lesbian and gay people was not even allowed to cross the public consciousness of Black america. We know in the 1980s, from documents gained through the Freedom of Information Act, that the FBI and CIA used our intolerance of difference to foment confusion and tragedy in segment after segment of Black communities of the 60s. Black was beautiful, but still suspect, and too often our forums for debate became stages for playing who's-Blacker-than-who or who's-poorer-than-who games, ones in which there can be no winners.

The 60s for me was a time of promise and excitement, but the 60s was also a time of isolation and frustration from within. It often felt like I was working and raising my children in a vacuum, and that it was my own fault — if I was only Blacker, things would be fine. It was a time of much wasted energy, and I was often in a lot of pain. Either I denied or chose between various aspects of my identity, or my work and my Blackness would be unacceptable. As a Black lesbian mother in an inter-racial marriage, there was usually some part of me guaranteed to offend everybody's comfortable prejudices of who I should be. That is how I learned that if I didn't define myself for myself, I would be crunched into other people's fantasies for me and eaten alive. My poetry, my life, my work, my energies for struggle were not acceptable unless I pretended to match somebody else's norm. I learned that not only couldn't I succeed at that game, but the energy needed for that masquerade would be lost to my work. And there were babies to raise, students to teach. The Vietnam War was escalating, our cities were burning, more and more of our school kids were nodding out in the halls, junk was overtaking our streets. We needed articulate power, not conformity. There were other strong Black workers whose visions were racked and silenced upon some imagined grid of narrow Blackness. Nor were Black women immune. At a national meeting of Black women for political action, a young civil rights activist who had been beaten and imprisoned in Mississippi only a few years before, was trashed and silenced as suspect because of her white husband. Some of us made it and some of us were lost to the struggle. It was a time of great hope and great expectation; it was also a time of great waste. That is history. We do not need to repeat these mistakes in the 80s.

The raw energy of Black determination released in the 60s powered changes in Black awareness and self-concepts and expectations. This energy is still being felt in movements for change among women, other peoples of Color, gays, the handicapped — among all the disenfranchised peoples of this society. That is a legacy of the 60s to ourselves and to others. But we must recognize that many of our high expectations of rapid revolutionary change did not in fact occur. And many of the gains that did are even now being dismantled. This is not a reason for despair, nor for rejection of the importance of those years. But we must face with clarity and insight the lessons to be learned from the oversimplification of any struggle for self-awareness and liberation, or we will not rally the force we need to face the multidimensional threats to our survival in the 80s.

There is no such thing as a single-issue struggle because we do not live single-issue lives. Malcolm knew this. Martin Luther King, Jr. knew this. Our struggles are particular, but we are not alone. We are not perfect, but we are stronger and wiser than the sum of our errors. Black people have been here before us and survived. We can read their lives like signposts on the road and find, as Bernice Reagon says so poignantly, that each one of us is here because somebody before us did something to make it possible. To learn from their mistakes is not to lessen our debt to them, nor to the hard work of becoming ourselves, and effective.

We lose our history so easily, what is not predigested for us by the *New York Times*, or the *Amsterdam News*, or *Time* magazine.

Maybe because we do not listen to our poets or to our fools, maybe because we do not listen to our mamas in ourselves. When I hear the deepest truths I speak coming out of my mouth sounding like my mother's, even remembering how I fought against her, I have to reassess both our relationship as well as the sources of my knowing. Which is not to say that I have to romanticize my mother in order to appreciate what she gave me — Woman, Black. We do not have to romanticize our past in order to be aware of how it seeds our present. We do not have to suffer the waste of an amnesia that robs us of the lessons of the past rather than permit us to read them with pride as well as deep understanding.

We know what it is to be lied to, and we know how important it is not to lie to ourselves.

We are powerful because we have survived, and that is what it is all about — survival and growth.

Within each one of us there is some piece of humanness that knows we are not being served by the machine which orchestrates crisis after crisis and is grinding all our futures into dust. If we are to keep the enormity of the forces aligned against us from establishing a false hierarchy of oppression, we must school ourselves to recognize that any attack against Blacks, any attack against women, is an attack against all of us who recognize that our interests are not being served by the systems we support. Each one of us here is a link in the connection between antipoor legislation, gay shootings, the burning of synagogues, street harassment, attacks against women, and resurgent violence against Black people. I ask myself as well as each one of you, exactly what alteration in the particular fabric of my everyday life does this connection call for? Survival is not a theory. In what way do I contribute to the subjugation of any part of those who I define as my people? Insight must illuminate the particulars of our lives: who labors to make the bread we waste, or the energy it takes to make nuclear poisons which will not biodegrade for one thousand years; or who goes blind assembling the microtransistors in our inexpensive calculators?

We are women trying to knit a future in a country where an Equal Rights Amendment was defeated as subversive legislation. We are Lesbians and gay men who, as the most obvious target of the New Right, are threatened with castration, imprisonment, and death in the streets. And we know that our erasure only paves the way for erasure of other people of Color, of the old, of the poor, of all of those who do not fit that mythic dehumanizing norm.

Can we really still afford to be fighting each other?

We are Black people living in a time when the consciousness of our intended slaughter is all around us. People of Color are increasingly expendable, our government's policy both here and abroad. We are functioning under a government ready to repeat in El Salvador and Nicaragua the tragedy of Vietnam, a government which stands on the wrong side of every single battle for liberation taking place upon this globe; a government which has invaded and conquered (as I edit this piece) the fifty-three square mile sovereign state of Grenada, under the pretext that her 110,000 people pose a threat to the U.S. Our papers are filled with supposed concern for human rights in white communist Poland while we sanction by acceptance and military supply the systematic genocide of apartheid in South Africa, of murder and torture in Haiti and El Salvador. American advisory teams bolster repressive governments across Central and South America, and in Haiti, while *advisory* is only a code name preceding military aid.

Decisions to cut aid for the terminally ill, for the elderly, for dependent children, for food stamps, even school lunches, are being made by men with full stomachs who live in comfortable houses with two cars and umpteen tax shelters. None of them go hungry to bed at night. Recently, it was suggested that senior citizens be hired to work in atomic plants because they are close to the end of their lives anyway.

Can any one of us here still afford to believe that efforts to reclaim the future can be private or individual? Can any one here still afford to believe that the pursuit of liberation can be the sole and particular province of any one particular race, or sex, or age, or religion, or sexuality, or class?

Revolution is not a one-time event. It is becoming always vigilant for the smallest opportunity to make a genuine change in established, outgrown responses; for instance, it is learning to address each other's difference with respect.

We share a common interest, survival, and it cannot be pursued in isolation from others simply because their differences make us uncomfortable. We know what it is to be lied to. The 60s should teach us how important it is not to lie to ourselves. Not to believe that revolution is a one-time event, or something that happens around us rather than inside of us. Not to believe that freedom can belong to any one group of us without the others also being free. How important it is not to allow even our leaders to define us to ourselves, or to define our sources of power to us.

There is no Black person here who can afford to wait to be led into positive action for survival. Each one of us must look clearly and closely at the genuine particulars (conditions) of his or her life and decide where action and energy is needed and where it can be effective. Change is the immediate responsibility of each of us, wherever and however we are standing, in whatever arena we choose. For while we wait for another Malcolm, another Martin, another charismatic Black leader to validate our struggles, old Black people are freezing to death in tenements, Black children are being brutalized and slaughtered in the streets, or lobotomized by television, and the percentage of Black families living below the poverty line is higher today than in 1963.

And if we wait to put our future into the hands of some new messiah, what will happen when those leaders are shot, or discredited, or tried for murder, or called homosexual, or otherwise disempowered? Do we put our future on hold? What is that internalized and self-destructive barrier that keeps us from moving, that keeps us from coming together?

We who are Black are at an extraordinary point of choice within our lives. To refuse to participate in the shaping of our future is to give it up. Do not be misled into passivity either by false security (they don't mean me) or by despair (there's nothing we can do). Each of us must find our work and do it. Militancy no longer means guns at high noon, if it ever did. It means actively working for change, sometimes in the absence of any surety that change is coming. It means doing the unromantic and tedious work necessary to forge meaningful coalitions, and it means recognizing which coalitions are possible and which coalitions are not. It means knowing that coalition, like unity, means the coming together of whole, self-actualized human beings, focused and believing, not fragmented automatons marching to a prescribed step. It means fighting despair.

And in the university, that is certainly no easy task, for each one of you by virtue of your being here will be deluged by opportunities to misname yourselves, to forget who you are, to forget where your real interests lie. Make no mistake, you will be courted; and nothing neutralizes creativity quicker than tokenism, that false sense of security fed by a myth of individual solutions. To paraphrase Malcolm — a Black woman attorney driving a Mercedes through Avenue Z in Brooklyn is still a "nigger bitch," two words which never seem to go out of style.

You do not have to be me in order for us to fight alongside each other. I do not have to be you to recognize that our wars are the same. What we must do is commit ourselves to some future that can include each other and to work toward that future with the particular strengths of our individual identities. And in order to do this, we must allow each other our differences at the same time as we recognize our sameness.

If our history has taught us anything, it is that action for change directed only against the external conditions of our oppressions is not enough. In order to be whole, we must recognize the despair oppression plants within each of us — that thin persistent voice that says our efforts are useless, it will never change, so why bother, accept it. And we must fight that inserted piece of self-destruction that lives and flourishes like a poison inside of us, unexamined until it makes us turn upon ourselves in each other. But we can put our finger down upon that loathing buried deep within each one of us and see who it encourages us to despise, and we can lessen its potency by the knowledge of our real connectedness, arcing across our differences.

Hopefully, we can learn from the 60s that we cannot afford to do our enemies' work by destroying each other.

What does it mean when an angry Black ballplayer — this happened in Illinois — curses a white heckler but pulls a knife on a Black one? What better way is there to police the streets of a minority community than to turn one generation against the other?

Referring to Black lesbians and gay men, the student president at Howard University says, on the occasion of a Gay Student Charter on campus, "The Black community has nothing to do with such filth — we will have to abandon *these people*." [italics mine] Abandon? Often without noticing, we absorb the racist belief that Black people are fitting targets for everybody's anger. We are closest to each other, and it is easier to vent fury upon each other than upon our enemies.

Of course, the young man at Howard was historically incorrect. As part of the Black community, he has a lot to do with "us." Some of our finest writers, organizers, artists and scholars in the 60s as well as today, have been lesbian and gay, and history will bear me out.

Over and over again in the 60s I was asked to justify my existence and my work, because I was a woman, because I was a Lesbian, because I was not a separatist, because some piece of me was not acceptable. Not because of my work but because of my identity. I had to learn to hold on to all the parts of me that served me, in spite of the pressure to express only one to the exclusion of all others. And I don't know what I'd say face to face with that young man at Howard University who says I'm filth because I identify women as my primary source of energy and support, except to say that it is my energy and the energy of other women very much like me which has contributed to his being where he is at this point. But I think he would not say it to my face because name-calling is always easiest when it is removed, academic. The move to render the presence of lesbians and gay men invisible in the intricate fabric of Black existence and survival is a move which contributes to fragmentation and weakness in the Black community.

In academic circles, as elsewhere, there is a kind of name-calling increasingly being used to keep young Black women in line. Often as soon as any young Black woman begins to recognize that she is oppressed as a woman as well as a Black, she is called a lesbian no matter how she identifies herself sexually. "What do you mean you don't want to make coffee take notes wash dishes go to bed with me, you a lesbian or something?" And at the threat of such a dreaded taint, all too often she falls meekly into line, however covertly. But the word *lesbian* is only threatening to those Black women who are intimidated by their sexuality, or who allow themselves to be defined by it and from outside themselves. Black women in struggle from our own perspective, speaking up for ourselves, sharing close ties with one another politically and emotionally, are not the enemies of Black men. We are Black women who seek our own definitions, recognizing diversity among ourselves with respect. We have been around within our communities for a very long time, and we have played pivotal parts in the survival of those communities: from Hat Shep Sut through Harriet Tubman to Daisy Bates and Fannie Lou Hamer to Lorraine Hansberry to your Aunt Maydine to some of you who sit before me now.

In the 60s Black people wasted a lot of our substance fighting each other. We cannot afford to do that in the 80s, when Washington, D.C. has the highest infant mortality rate of any U.S. city, 60 percent of the Black community under twenty is unemployed and more are becoming unemployable, lynchings are on the increase, and less than half the registered Black voters voted in the last election.

How are you practicing what you preach — whatever you preach, and who exactly is listening? As Malcolm stressed, we are not responsible for our oppression, but we must be responsible for our own liberation. It is not going to be easy, but we have what we have learned and what we have been given that is useful. We have the power those who came before us have given us, to move beyond the place where they were standing. We have the trees, and water, and sun, and our children. Malcolm X does not live in the dry texts of his words as we read them; he lives in the energy we generate and use to move along the visions we share with him. We are making the future as well as bonding to survive the enormous pressures of the present, and that is what it means to be a part of history.

Eye to Eye: Black Women, Hatred, and Anger*

*Where does the pain go when it goes away?***

EVERY BLACK WOMAN in America lives her life somewhere along a wide curve of ancient and unexpressed angers.

My Black woman's anger is a molten pond at the core of me, my most fiercely guarded secret. I know how much of my life as a powerful feeling woman is laced through with this net of rage. It is an electric thread woven into every emotional tapestry upon which I set the essentials of my life — a boiling hot spring likely to erupt at any point, leaping out of my consciousness like a fire on the landscape. How to train that anger with accuracy rather than deny it has been one of the major tasks of my life.

Other Black women are not the root cause nor the source of that pool of anger. I know this, no matter what the particular situation may be between me and another Black woman at the moment. Then why does that anger unleash itself most tellingly against another Black woman at the least excuse? Why do I judge her in a more critical light than any other, becoming enraged when she does not measure up?

---

* An abbreviated version of this essay was published in *Essence*, vol. 14, no. 6 (October 1983). I wish to thank the following women without whose insights and support I could not have completed this paper: Andrea Canaan, Frances Clayton, Michelle Cliff, Blanche Wiesen Cook, Clare Coss, Yvonne Flowers, Gloria Joseph, Adrienne Rich, Charlotte Sheedy, Judy Simmons and Barbara Smith. This paper is dedicated to the memory of Sheila Blackwell Pinckney, 1953-1983.

** From a poem by Dr. Gloria Joseph.

And if behind the object of my attack should lie the face of my own self, unaccepted, then what could possibly quench a fire fueled by such reciprocating passions?

When I started to write about the intensity of the angers between Black women, I found I had only begun to touch one tip of a three-pronged iceberg, the deepest understructure of which was Hatred, that societal deathwish directed against us from the moment we were born Black and female in America. From that moment on we have been steeped in hatred — for our color, for our sex, for our effrontery in daring to presume we had any right to live. As children we absorbed that hatred, passed it through ourselves, and for the most part, we still live our lives outside of the recognition of what that hatred really is and how it functions. Echoes of it return as cruelty and anger in our dealings with each other. For each of us bears the face that hatred seeks, and we have each learned to be at home with cruelty because we have survived so much of it within our own lives.

Before I can write about Black women's anger, I must write about the poisonous seepage of hatred that fuels that anger, and of the cruelty that is spawned when they meet.

I have found this out by scrutinizing my own expectations of other Black women, by following the threads of my own rage at Blackwomanness back into the hatred and despisal that embroidered my life with fire long before I knew where that hatred came from, or why it was being heaped upon me. Children know only themselves as reasons for the happenings in their lives. So of course as a child I decided there must be something terribly wrong with me that inspired such contempt. The bus driver didn't look at other people like that. All the things my mother had warned me not to do and be that I had gone right ahead and done and been must be to blame.

To search for power within myself means I must be willing to move through being afraid to whatever lies beyond. If I look at my most vulnerable places and acknowledge the pain I have felt, I can remove the source of that pain from my enemies' arsenals. My history cannot be used to feather my enemies' arrows then, and that lessens their power over me. Nothing I accept about myself can be used against me to diminish me. I am who I am, doing what I came to do, acting upon you like a drug or a chisel to remind you of your me-ness, as I discover you in myself.

America's measurement of me has lain like a barrier across the realization of my own powers. It was a barrier which I had to examine and dismantle, piece by painful piece, in order to use my energies fully and creatively. It is easier to deal with the external manifestations of racism and sexism than it is to deal with the results of those distortions internalized within our consciousness of ourselves and one another.

But what is the nature of that reluctance to connect with each other on any but the most superficial levels? What is the source of that mistrust and distance maintained between Black women?

I don't like to talk about hate. I don't like to remember the cancellation and hatred, heavy as my wished-for death, seen in the eyes of so many white people from the time I could see. It was echoed in newspapers and movies and holy pictures and comic books and Amos 'n Andy radio programs. I had no tools to dissect it, no language to name it.

The AA subway train to Harlem. I clutch my mother's sleeve, her arms full of shopping bags, christmas-heavy. The wet smell of winter clothes, the train's lurching. My mother spots an almost seat, pushes my little snowsuited body down. On one side of me a man reading a paper. On the other, a woman in a fur hat staring at me. Her mouth twitches as she stares and then her gaze drops down, pulling mine with it. Her leather-gloved hand plucks at the line where my new blue snowpants and her sleek fur coat meet. She jerks her coat closer to her. I look. I do not see whatever terrible thing she is seeing on the seat between us — probably a roach. But she has communicated her horror to me. It must be something very bad from the way she's looking, so I pull my snowsuit closer to me away from it, too. When I look up the woman is still staring at me, her nose holes and eyes huge. And suddenly I realize there is nothing crawling up the seat between us; it is me she doesn't want her coat to touch. The fur brushes past my face as she stands with a shudder and holds on to a strap in the speeding train. Born and bred a New York City child, I quickly slide over to make room for my mother to sit down. No word has been spoken. I'm afraid to say anything to my mother because I don't know what I've done. I look at the sides of my snowpants, secretly. Is there something on them? Something's going on here I do not understand, but I will never forget it. Her eyes. The flared nostrils. The hate.

My three-year-old eyes ache from the machinery used to test them. My forehead is sore. I have been poked and prodded in the eyes and stared into all morning. I huddle into the tall metal and leather chair, frightened and miserable and wanting my mother. On the other side of the eye clinic's examining room, a group of young white men in white coats discuss my peculiar eyes. Only one voice remains in my memory. "From the looks of her she's probably simple, too." They all laugh. One of them comes over to me, enunciating slowly and carefully, "OK, girlie, go wait outside now." He pats me on the cheek. I am grateful for the absence of harshness.

The Story Hour librarian reading *Little Black Sambo*. Her white fingers hold up the little book about a shoebutton-faced little boy with big red lips and many pigtails and a hatful of butter. I remember the pictures hurting me and my thinking again there must be something wrong with me because everybody else is laughing and besides the library downtown has given this little book a special prize, the library lady tells us.

SO WHAT'S WRONG WITH YOU, ANYWAY? DON'T BE SO *SENSITIVE!*

Sixth grade in a new catholic school and I am the first Black student. The white girls laugh at my braided hair. The nun sends a note home to my mother saying that "pigtails are not appropriate attire for school," and that I should learn to comb my hair in "a more becoming style."

Lexie Goldman and I on Lexington Avenue, our adolescent faces flushed from springtime and our dash out of high school. We stop at a luncheonette, ask for water. The woman behind the counter smiles at Lexie. Gives us water. Lexie's in a glass. Mine in a paper cup. Afterward we joke about mine being portable. Too loudly.

My first interview for a part-time job after school. An optical company on Nassau Street has called my school and asked for one of its students. The man behind the counter reads my application and then looks up at me, surprised by my Black face. His eyes remind me of the woman on the train when I was five. Then something else is added, as he looks me up and down, pausing at my breasts.

My light-skinned mother kept me alive within an environment where my life was not a high priority. She used whatever methods she had at hand, few as they were. She never talked about color. My mother was a very brave woman, born in the West Indies, unprepared for america. And she disarmed me with her silences. Somewhere I knew it was a lie that nobody else noticed color. Me, darker than my two sisters. My father, darkest of all. I was always jealous of my sisters because my mother thought they were such good girls, whereas I was bad, always in trouble. "Full of the devil," she used to say. They were neat, I was untidy. They were quiet, I was noisy. They were well-behaved, I was rowdy. They took piano lessons and won prizes in deportment. I stole money from my father's pockets and broke my ankle sledding downhill. They were good-looking, I was dark. Bad, mischievous, a born troublemaker if ever there was one.

Did *bad* mean *Black*? The endless scrubbing with lemon juice in the cracks and crevices of my ripening, darkening, body. And oh, the sins of my dark elbows and knees, my gums and nipples, the folds of my neck and the cave of my armpits!

The hands that grab at me from behind the stairwell are Black hands. Boys' hands, punching, rubbing, pinching, pulling at my dress. I hurl the garbage bag I'm carrying into the ashcan and jerk away, fleeing back upstairs. Hoots follow me. "That's right, you better run, you ugly yaller bitch, just wait!" Obviously, color was relative.

My mother taught me to survive from a very early age by her own example. Her silences also taught me isolation, fury, mistrust, self-rejection, and sadness. My survival lay in learning how to use the weapons she gave me, also, to fight against those things within myself, unnamed.

And survival is the greatest gift of love. Sometimes, for Black mothers, it is the only gift possible, and tenderness gets lost. My mother bore me into life as if etching an angry message into marble. Yet I survived the hatred around me because my mother made me know, by oblique reference, that no matter what went on at home, outside shouldn't oughta be the way it was. But since it was that way outside, I moved in a fen of unexplained anger that encircled me and spilled out against whomever was closest that shared those hated selves. Of course I did not realize it at the time. That anger lay like a pool of acid deep inside me, and whenever I felt deeply, I felt it, attaching itself in the strangest places. Upon those as powerless as I. My first friend asking, "Why do you go around hitting all the time? Is that the only way you know how to be friends?

What other creature in the world besides the Black woman has had to build the knowledge of so much hatred into her survival and keep going?

It is shortly after the Civil War. In a greystone hospital on 110th Street in New York City a woman is screaming. She is Black, and healthy, and has been brought here from the South. I do not know her name. Her baby is ready to be born. But her legs have been tied together out of a curiosity masquerading as science. Her baby births itself to death against her bone.

Where are you seven-year-old Elizabeth Eckford of Little Rock, Arkansas? It is a bright Monday morning and you are on your way to your first day of school, draped in spittle, white hatred running down your pink sweater and a white mother's twisted mouth working — savage, inhuman — wide over your jaunty braids held high by their pink ribbons.

Numvulo has walked five days from the bleak place where the lorry deposited her. She stands in the Capetown, South Africa rain, her bare feet in the bulldozer tracks where her house once was. She picks up a piece of soaked cardboard that once covered her table and holds it over the head of her baby strapped to her back. Soon she will be arrested and taken back to the reserve, where she does not even speak the language. She will never get permission to live near her husband.

The bicentennial, in Washington, D.C. Two ample Black women stand guard over household belonging piled haphazardly onto a sidewalk in front of a house. Furniture, toys, bundles of clothes. One woman absently rocks a toy horse with the toe of her shoe, back and forth. Across the street on the side of a building opposite is a sign painted in story-high black letters, *GOD HATES YOU*.

Addie Mae Collins, Carol Robertson, Cynthia Wesley, Denise McNair. Four little Black girls, none more than ten years of age, singing their last autumn song in a Sunday church school in Birmingham, Alabama. After the explosion clears it is not possible to tell which patent leather Sunday shoe belongs to which found leg.

What other human being absorbs so much virulent hostility and still functions?

Black women have a history of the use and sharing of power, from the Amazon legions of Dahomey through the Ashanti warrior queen Yaa Asantewaa and the freedom fighter Harriet Tubman, to the economically powerful market-women guilds of present West Africa. We have a tradition of closeness and mutual care and support, from the all-woman courts of the Queen Mothers of Benin to the present-day Sisterhood of the Good Death, a community of old women in Brazil who, as escaped slaves, provided escape and refuge for other enslaved women, and who now care for each other.*

We are Black women born into a society of entrenched loathing and contempt for whatever is Black and female. We are strong and enduring. We are also deeply scarred. As African women together, we once made the earth fertile with our fingers. We can make the earth bear as well as mount the first line of fire in defense of the King. And having killed, in his

* Unpublished paper by Samella Lewis.

name and in our own (Harriet's rifle speaks, shouldered in the grim marsh), we still know that the power to kill is less than the power to create, for it produces an ending rather than the beginning of something new.

Anger – a passion of displeasure that may be excessive or misplaced but not necessarily harmful. Hatred – an emotional habit or attitude of mind in which aversion is coupled with ill will. Anger, used, does not destroy. Hatred does.

Racism and sexism are grown-up words. Black children in america cannot avoid these distortions in their living and, too often, do not have the words for naming them. But both are correctly perceived as hatred.

Growing up, metabolizing hatred like a daily bread. Because I am Black, because I am woman, because I am not Black enough, because I am not some particular fantasy of a woman, because I AM. On such a consistent diet, one can eventually come to value the hatred of one's enemies more than one values the love of friends, for that hatred becomes the source of anger, and anger is a powerful fuel.

And true, sometimes it seems that anger alone keeps me alive; it burns with a bright and undiminished flame. Yet anger, like guilt, is an incomplete form of human knowledge. More useful than hatred, but still limited. Anger is useful to help clarify our differences, but in the long run, strength that is bred by anger alone is a blind force which cannot create the future. It can only demolish the past. Such strength does not focus upon what lies ahead, but upon what lies behind, upon what created it – hatred. And hatred is a deathwish for the hated, not a lifewish for anything else.

To grow up metabolizing hatred like daily bread means that eventually every human interaction becomes tainted with the negative passion and intensity of its by-products – anger and cruelty.

We are African women and we know, in our blood's telling, the tenderness with which our foremothers held each other. It is that connection which we are seeking. We have the stories of Black women who healed each other's wounds, raised each other's children, fought each other's battles, tilled each other's earth, and eased each other's passages into life and into death. We know the possibilities of support and connection for which we all yearn, and about which we dream so often. We have a growing Black women's literature which is richly evocative of these possibilities and connections. But connections between Black women are not automatic by virtue of our similarities, and the possibilities of genuine communication between us are not easily achieved.

Often we give lip service to the idea of mutual support and connection between Black women because we have not yet crossed the barriers to these possibilities, nor fully explored the angers and fears that keep us from realizing the power of a real Black sisterhood. And to acknowledge our dreams is to sometimes acknowledge the distance between those dreams and our present situation. Acknowledged, our dreams can shape the realities of our future, if we arm them with the hard work and scrutiny of now. We cannot settle for the pretenses of connection, or for parodies of self-love. We cannot continue to evade each other on the deepest levels because we fear each other's angers, nor continue to believe that respect means never looking directly nor with openness into another Black woman's eyes.

*I was not meant to be alone and without you who understand.**

I.

I know the anger that lies inside of me like I know the beat of my heart and the taste of my spit. It is easier to be angry than to hurt. Anger is what I do best. It is easier to be furious than to be yearning. Easier to crucify myself in you than to take on the threatening universe of whiteness by admitting that we are worth wanting each other.

As Black women, we have shared so many similar experiences. Why doesn't this commonality bring us closer together instead of setting us at each other's throats with weapons well-honed by familiarity?

---

* From "Letters from Black Feminists, 1972-1978" by Barbara Smith and Beverly Smith in *Conditions: Four* (1979).

The anger with which I meet another Black woman's slightest deviation from my immediate need or desire or concept of a proper response is a deep and hurtful anger, chosen only in the sense of a choice of desperation — reckless through despair. That anger which masks my pain that we are so separate who should most be together — my pain — that she could perhaps not need me as much as I need her, or see me through the blunted eye of the haters, that eye I know so well from my own distorted images of her. Erase or be erased!

I stand in the Public Library waiting to be recognized by the Black woman library clerk seated a few feet behind the desk. She seems engrossed in a book, beautiful in her youth and self-assuredness. I straighten my glasses, giving a tiny shake to my bangles in the process just in case she has not seen me, but I somehow know she has. Otherwise motionless, she slowly turns her head and looks up. Her eyes cross mine with a look of such incidental hostility that I feel pilloried to the wall. Two male patrons enter behind me. At that, she rises and moves toward me. "Yes," she says, with no inflection at all, her eyes carefully elsewhere. I've never seen this young woman before in my life. I think to myself, "now that's what you call an attitude," recognizing the rising tension inside of me.

The art, beyond insolence, of the Black girl's face as she cuts her elegant sidelong glance at me. What makes her eyes slide off of mine? What does she see that angers her so, or infuriates her, or disgusts her? Why do I want to break her face off when her eyes do not meet mine? Why does she wear my sister's face? My daughter's mouth turned down about to suck itself in? The eyes of a furious and rejected lover? Why do I dream I cradle you at night? Divide your limbs between the food bowls of my least favorite animals? Keep vigil for you night after terrible night, wondering? Oh sister, where is that dark rich land we wanted to wander through together?

Hate said the voice wired in 3/4 time printed in dirty type all the views fit to kill, me and you, me or you. And whose future image have we destroyed — your face or mine — without either how shall I look again at both — lacking either is lacking myself.

And if I trust you what pale dragon will you feed our brown flesh to from fear, self-preservation, or to what brothered altar all innocent of loving that has no place to go and so becomes another face of terror or of hate?

A dumb beast endlessly recording inside the poisonous attacks of silence — meat gone wrong — what could ever grow in that dim lair and how does the child convert from sacrifice to liar?

My blood sister, across her living room from me. Sitting back in her chair while I talk earnestly, trying to reach her, trying to alter the perceptions of me that cause her so much pain. Slowly, carefully, and coldly, so I will not miss one single scathing word, she says, "I am not interested in understanding whatever you're trying to say — I don't care to hear it."

I have never gotten over the anger that you did not want me as a sister, nor an ally, nor even a diversion one cut above the cat. You have never gotten over the anger that I appeared at all. And that I am different, but not different enough. One woman has eyes like my sister who never forgave me for appearing before she had a chance to win her mother's love, as if anybody ever could. Another woman wears the high cheekbones of my other sister who wanted to lead but had only been taught to obey, so now she is dedicated to ruling by obedience, a passive vision.

Who did we expect the other to be who is not yet at peace with our own selves? I cannot shut you out the way I shut the others out so maybe I can destroy you. Must destroy you?

We do not love ourselves, therefore we cannot love each other. Because we see in each other's face our own face, the face we never stopped wanting. Because we survived and survival breeds desire for more self. A face we never stopped wanting at the same time as we try to obliterate it.

Why don't we meet each other's eyes? Do we expect betrayal in each other's gaze, or recognition?

If just once we were to feel the pain of all Black women's blood flooding up to drown us! I stayed afloat buoyed by an anger so deep at my loneliness that I could only move toward further survival.

When one cannot influence a situation it is an act of wisdom to withdraw.*

Every Black woman in america has survived several lifetimes of hatred, where even in the candy store cases of our childhood, little brown niggerbaby candies testified against us. We survived the wind-driven spittle on our child's shoe and pink flesh-colored bandaids, attempted rapes on rooftops and the prodding fingers of the super's boy, seeing our girlfriends blown to bits in Sunday School, and we absorbed that loathing as a natural state. We had to metabolize such hatred that our cells have learned to live upon it because we had to, or die of it. Old King Mithridates learned to eat arsenic bit by bit and so outwitted his poisoners, but I'd have hated to kiss him upon his lips! Now we deny such hatred ever existed because we have learned to neutralize it through ourselves, and the catabolic process throws off waste products of fury even when we love.

> *I see hatred*
> *I am bathed in it, drowning in it*
> *since almost the beginning of my life*
> *it has been the air I breathe*
> *the food I eat, the content of my perceptions;*
> *the single most constant fact of my existence*
> *is their hatred . . .*
> *I am too young for my history***

It is not that Black women shed each other's psychic blood so easily, but that we have ourselves bled so often, the pain of bloodshed becomes almost commonplace. If I have learned to eat my own flesh in the forest — starving, keening, learning the lesson of the she-wolf who chews off her own paw to leave the trap behind — if I must drink my own blood, thirsting, why should I stop at yours until your dear dead arms hang like withered garlands upon my breast and I weep for your going, oh my sister, I grieve for our gone.

When an error of oversight allows one of us to escape without the full protective dose of fury and air of contemptuous disdain,

---

* From *The I Ching*.

** From "Nigger" by Judy Dothard Simmons in *Decent Intentions* (Blind Beggar Press, P.O. Box 437, Williamsbridge Station, Bronx, New York 10467, 1983).

when she approaches us without a measure of distrust and reserve flowing from her pores, or without her eyes coloring each appraisal of us with that unrelenting sharpness and suspicion reserved only for each other, when she approaches without sufficient caution, then she is cursed by the first accusation of derision – *naive* – meaning not programmed for defensive attack before inquiry. Even more than *confused, naive* is the ultimate wipeout between us.

Black women eating our own hearts out for nourishment in an empty house empty compound empty city in an empty season, and for each of us one year the spring will not return – we learned to savor the taste of our own flesh before any other because that was all that was allowed us. And we have become to each other unmentionably dear and immeasurably dangerous. I am writing about an anger so huge and implacable, so corrosive, it must destroy what it most needs for its own solution, dissolution, resolution. Here we are attempting to address each others' eyes directly. Even if our words taste sharp as the edge of a lost woman's voice, we are speaking.

II

A Black woman, working her years, committed to life as she lives it, the children fed and clothed and loved as she can into some strength that does not allow them to encyst like horse chestnuts, knowing all the time from the start that she must either kill them or eventually send them into the deathlands, the white labyrinth.

I sat at our Thanksgiving Day table listening to my daughter talk about the university and the horrors of determined invisibility. Over the years I have recorded her dreams of death at their hands, sometimes glorious, sometimes cheap. She tells me of the teachers who refuse to understand simple questions, who look at her as if she were a benign – meaning powerless – but unsightly tumor. She weeps. I hold her. I tell her to remember the university doesn't own her, that she has a home. But I have let her go into that jungle of ghosts, having taught her only how to be fleet of foot, how to whistle, how to love, and how not to run. Unless she has to. It is never enough.

Black women give our children forth into a hatred that seared our own young days with bewilderment, hoping we have taught them something they can use to fashion their own new and less costly pathways to survival. Knowing I did not slit their throats at birth tear out the tiny beating heart with my own despairing teeth the way some sisters did in the slaveships chained to corpses and therefore was I committed to this very moment.

*The price of increasing power is increasing opposition.**

I sat listening to my girl talk about the bent world she was determined to reenter in spite of all she was saying, because she views a knowledge of that world as part of an arsenal which she can use to change it all. I listened, hiding my pained need to snatch her back into the web of my smaller protections. I sat watching while she worked it out bit by hurtful bit — what she really wanted — feeling her rage wax and wane, feeling her anger building against me because I could not help her do it nor do it for her, nor would she allow that.

All mothers see their daughters leaving. Black mothers see it happening as a sacrifice through the veil of hatred hung like sheets of lava in the pathway before their daughters. All daughters see their mothers leaving. Black girls see it happening through a veil of threatened isolation no fire of trusting pierces.

Last month I held another Black woman in my arms as she sobbed out the grief and deprivation of her mother's death. Her inconsolable loss — the emptiness of the emotional landscape she was seeing in front of her — spoke out of her mouth from a place of untouchable aloneness that could never admit another Black woman close enough again to matter. "The world is divided into two kinds of people," she said, "those who have mothers and those who don't. And I don't have a mother anymore." What I heard her saying was that no other Black woman would ever see who she was, ever trust or be trusted by her again. I heard in her cry of loneliness the source of the romance between Black women and our mommas.

---

* From *The I Ching.*

Little Black girls, tutored by hate into wanting to become anything else. We cut our eyes at sister because she can only reflect what everybody else except momma seemed to know — that we were hateful, or ugly, or worthless, but certainly unblessed. We were not boys and we were not white, so we counted for less than nothing, except to our mommas.

If we can learn to give ourselves the recognition and acceptance that we have come to expect only from our mommas, Black women will be able to see each other much more clearly and deal with each other much more directly.

I think about the harshness that exists so often within the least encounter between Black women, the judgment and the sizing up, that cruel refusal to connect. I know sometimes I feel like it is worth my life to disagree with another Black woman. Better to ignore her, withdraw from her, go around her, just don't deal with her. Not just because she irritates me, but because she might destroy me with the cruel force of her response to what must feel like an affront, namely me. Or I might destroy her with the force of mine, for the very same reason. The fears are equal.

Once I can absorb the particulars of my life as a Black woman, and multiply them by my two children and all the days of our collective Black lives, and I do not falter beneath the weight — what Black woman is not a celebration, like water, like sunlight, like rock — is it any wonder that my voice is harsh? Now to require of myself the effort of awareness, so that harshness will not function in the places it is least deserved — toward my sisters.

Why do Black women reserve a particular voice of fury and disappointment for each other? Who is it we must destroy when we attack each other with that tone of predetermined and correct annihilation? We reduce one another to our own lowest common denominator, and then we proceed to try and obliterate what we most desire to love and touch, the problematic self, unclaimed but fiercely guarded from the other.

This cruelty between us, this harshness, is a piece of the legacy of hate with which we were inoculated from the time we were born by those who intended it to be an injection of death. But we adapted, learned to take it in and use it, unscrutinized. Yet at what cost! In order to withstand the weather, we had to become stone, and now we bruise ourselves upon the other who is closest.

How do I alter course so each Black woman's face I meet is not the face of my mother or my killer?

I loved you. I dreamed about you. I talked to you for hours in my sleep sitting under a silk-cotton tree our arms around each other or braiding each other's hair or oiling each other's backs, and every time I run into you on the street or at the post office or behind the Medicaid desk I want to wring your neck.

There are so many occasions in each of our lives for righteous fury, multiplied and dividing.

• Black women being told that we can be somehow better, and are worse, but never equal. To Black men. To other women. To human beings.

• The white academic feminist who tells me she is so glad *This Bridge Called My Back** exists, because now it gives her a chance to deal with racism without having to face the harshness of Black undiluted by other colors. What she means is she does not have to examine her own specific terror and loathing of Blackness, nor deal with the angers of Black women. So get away with your dirty ugly mean faces, all screwed up all the time!

• The racist filmstrip artist who I thought I had handled so patiently and well. I didn't blow up his damned machine. I explained how his racial blindness made me feel and how his film could be altered to have some meaning. He probably learned something about showing Black images. Then I came home and almost tore up my house and my lover because some invitations happened to be misprinted. Not seeing where the charge of rage was born.

• A convicted Black man, a torturer of women and children, army-trained to be a killer, writes in his journal in his death cell:

* *This Bridge Called My Back: Writings by Radical Women of Color* edited by Cherríe Moraga and Gloria Anzaldua (Kitchen Table: Women of Color Press, New York, 1984).

"I am the type of person you are most likely to find driving a Mercedes and sitting in the executive offices of 100 big corporations." And he's right. Except he's Black.

How do we keep from releasing our angers at them upon ourselves and each other? How do I free myself from this poison I was force-fed like a Strasburg goose until I vomited anger at the least scent of anything nourishing, *oh my sister the belligerent lift of your shoulder the breath of your hair* . . . . We each learned the craft of destruction. It is all they knew to allow us, yet look how our words are finding each other again.

It is difficult to construct a wholesomeness model when we are surrounded with synonyms for filth. But not impossible. We have, after all, survived for a reason. (How do I define my impact upon this earth?) I begin by searching for the right questions.

Dear Leora,

For two Black women to enter an analytic or therapeutic relationship means beginning an essentially uncharted and insecure journey. There are no prototypes, no models, no objectively accessible body of experience other than ourselves by which to examine the specific dynamics of our interactions as Black women. Yet this interaction can affect all the other psychic matter attended profoundly. It is to scrutinize that very interaction that I sought you out professionally, and I have come to see that it means picking my way through our similarities and our differences, as well as through our histories of calculated mistrust and desire.

Because it has not been done before or at least not been noted, this particular scrutiny is painful and fraught with the vulnerability of all psychic scrutinies plus all of the pitfalls created by our being Black women in a white male world, and Black women who have survived. This is a scrutiny often sidestepped or considered unimportant or beside the point. EXAMPLE: I can't tell you how many good white psychwomen have said to me, "Why should it matter if I am Black or white?" who would never think of saying, "Why does it matter if I am female or male?" EX-AMPLE: I don't know who you are in supervision with, but I can bet it's not with another Black woman.

So this territory between us feels new and frightening as well as urgent, rigged with detonating pieces of our own individual racial histories which neither of us chose but which each of us bears the scars from. And those are particular to each of us. But there is a history which we share because we are Black women in a racist sexist cauldron, and that means some part of this journey is yours, also.

I have many troubled areas of self that will be neither new nor problematic to you as a trained and capable psychperson. I think you are a brave woman and I respect that, yet I doubt that your training can have prepared you to explore the tangle of need, fear, distrust, despair, and hope which operates between us, and certainly not to the depth necessary. Because neither of us is male nor white, we belong to a group of human beings that has not been thought worthy of that kind of study. So we have only who we are, with or without the courage to use those selves for further exploration and clarification of how what lies between us as Black women affects us and the work we do together.

Yet if we do not do it here between us, each one of us will have to do it somewhere else, sometime.

I know these things: I do not yet know what to do about them. But I do want to make them fit together to serve my life and my work, and I don't mean merely in a way that feels safe. I don't know how they can further and illuminate your life and work, but I know they can. It is sometimes both the curse and the blessing of the poet to perceive without yet being able to order those perceptions, and that is another name for Chaos.

But of course it is out of Chaos that new worlds are born.

I look forward to our meeting eye to eye.

Audre

III

There has been so much death and loss around me recently, without metaphor or redeeming symbol, that sometimes I feel trapped into one idiom only – that one of suffering and its codicil, to bear. The same problem exists with anger. I have processed too much of it recently, or else the machinery is slowing down or becoming less efficient, and it creeps into my most crucial interchanges.

Perhaps this is why it is often easier for Black women to interact with white women, even though those interactions are often a dead end emotionally. For with white women there is a middle depth of interaction possible and sustainable, an emotional limit to relationships of self upon self acknowledged.

Now why is this not so with Frances, who is white, and whom I meet at a depth beyond anyone? When I speak of Frances and me I am talking about a relationship not only of great depth but one of great breadth also, a totaling of differences without merging. I am also speaking of a love shaped by our mutual commitment to hard work and confrontation over many years, each of us refusing to settle for what was easy, or simple, or acceptably convenient.

That middle depth of relationship more usually possible between Black and white women, however, is less threatening than the tangle of unexplored needs and furies that face any two Black women who seek to engage each other directly, emotionally, no matter what the context of their relationship may be. This holds true for office workers and political activists as well as lovers. But it is through threading this tangle that new visions of self and possibility between Black women emerge. Again, I am speaking here of social relationships, for it is crucial that we examine dynamics between women who are not lovers as well as between women who are.

I ask myself, do I ever use my war against racism to avoid other even more unanswerable pain? And if so, doesn't that make the energy behind my battles against racism sometimes more tenuous, or less clearheaded, or subject to unexpected stresses and disappointments? White people can never truly validate us. For example: At this point in time, were racism to be totally eradicated from those middle range relationships between Black women and white women, those relationships might become deeper, but they would still never satisfy our particular Black woman's need for one another, given our shared knowledge and traditions and history. There are two very different struggles involved here. One is the war against racism in white people, and the other is the need for Black women to confront and wade through the racist constructs underlying our deprivation of each other. And these battles are not at all the same.

But sometimes it feels like better a righteous fury than the dull ache of loss, loss, loss. My daughter leaving her time of daughterhood. Friends going away in one way or another.

. . . *as those seemingly alike mature, nature emphasizes their uniqueness and the differences become more obvious.**

How often have I demanded from another Black woman what I had not dared to give myself — acceptance, faith, enough space to consider change? How often have I asked her to leap across difference, suspicion, distrust, old pain? How many times have I expected her to jump the hideous gaps of our learned despisals alone, like an animal trained through blindness to ignore the precipice? How many times have I forgotten to ask this question?

Am I not reaching out for you in the only language I know? Are you reaching for me in your only salvaged tongue? If I try to hear yours across our differences does/will that mean you can hear mine?

Do we explore these questions or do we settle for that secret isolation which is the learned tolerance of deprivation of each other — that longing for each other's laughter, dark ease, sharing, and permission to be ourselves that we do not admit to feeling, usually, because then we would have to admit the lack; and the pain of that lacking, persistent as a low-grade fever and as debilitating?

Do we reenact these crucifixions upon each other, the avoidance, the cruelty, the judgments, because we have not

---

* From *The I Ching.*

been allowed Black goddesses, Black heroines; because we have not been allowed to see our mothers and our selves in their/our own magnificence until that magnificence became part of our blood and bone? One of the functions of hatred is certainly to mask and distort the beauty which is power in ourselves.

I am hungry for Black women who will not turn from me in anger and contempt even before they know me or hear what I have to say. I am hungry for Black women who will not turn away from me even if they do not agree with what I say. We are, after all, talking about different combinations of the same borrowed sounds.

Sometimes exploring our differences feels like marching out to war. I hurl myself with trepidation into the orbit of every Black woman I want to reach, advancing with the best of what I have to offer held out at arms length before me — myself. Does it feel different to her? At the same time as I am terrified, expecting betrayal, rejection, the condemnations of laughter, is she feeling judged by me?

Most of the Black women I know think I cry too much, or that I'm too public about it. I've been told that crying makes me seem soft and therefore of little consequence. As if our softness *has* to be the price we pay out for power, rather than simply the one that's paid most easily and most often.

I fight nightmare images inside my own self, see them, own them, know they did not destroy me before and will not destroy me now if I speak them out, admit how they have scarred me, that my mother taught me to survive at the same time as she taught me to fear my own Blackness. "Don't trust white people because they mean us no good and don't trust anyone darker than you because their hearts are as Black as their faces." (And where did that leave me, the darkest one?) It is painful even now to write it down. How many messages like that come down to all of us, and in how many different voices, how many different ways? And how can we expunge these messages from our consciousness without first recognizing what it was they were saying, and how destructive they were?

IV

What does it take to be tough? Learned cruelty?

Now there is bound to be a voice saying that Black women have always helped one another, haven't we? And that is the paradox of our inner conflict. We have a strong and ancient tradition of bonding and mutual support, and the memorized threads of that tradition exist within each of us, in opposition to the anger and suspicion engendered by self-hate.

When the world moved against me with a disapproving frown / It was sister put the ground back under my feet.*

Hearing those words sung has always provoked the most profound and poignant sense of loss within me for something I wanted to feel and could not because it had never happened for me. There are some Black women for whom it has. For others of us, that sense of being able to depend upon rock bottom support from our sisters is something we dream about and work toward, knowing it is possible, but also very problematic across the realities of fear and suspicion lying between us.

Our anger, tempered over survival fires, shuttered behind downcast eyelids, or else blazing out of our eyes at the oddest times. Looking up from between the legs of a lover, over a notebook in the middle of a lecture and I almost lost my train of thought, ringing up groceries in the supermarket, filling out the form behind the unemployment office window, stepping out of a cab in the middle of Broadway on the arm of a businessman from Lagos, sweeping ahead of me into a shop as I open the door, looking into each other's eyes for a split second only — furious, cutting, sisters. My daughter asking me all the time when she was a little girl, "Are you angry about something, Mommy?"

As Black women, we have wasted our angers too often, buried them, called them someone else's, cast them wildly into oceans of racism and sexism from which no vibration resounded, hurled them into each other's teeth and then ducked to avoid the impact. But by and large, we avoid open expression of them,

---

* From "Every Woman Ever Loved A Woman" by Bernice Johnson Reagon, song performed by Sweet Honey in the Rock.

or cordon them off in a rigid and unapproachable politeness. The rage that feels illicit or unjustified is kept secret, unnamed, and preserved forever. We are stuffed with furies, against ourselves, against each other, terrified to examine them lest we find ourselves in bold print fingered and named what we have always felt and even sometimes preferred ourselves to be — alone. And certainly, there are enough occasions in all our lives where we can use our anger righteously, enough for many lifetimes. We can avoid confrontation with each other very readily. It is so much easier to examine our anger within situations that are (relatively) clearcut and emotionally unloaded. It is so much easier to express our anger in those middle depth relationships that do not threaten genuine self-exposure. And yet always that hunger for the substance known, a hunger for the real shared, for the sister who shares.

It is hard to stand up in the teeth of white dismissal and aggression, of gender hatred and attack. It is so much harder to tackle face-on the rejection of Black women who may be seeing in my face some face they have not discarded in their own mirror, who see in my eyes the shape they have come to fear may be their own. So often this fear is stoked between Black women by the feared loss of a male companion, present or sought after. For we have also been taught that a man acquired was the sole measure of success, and yet they almost never stay.

One Black woman sits and silently judges another, how she looks, how she acts, how she impresses others. The first woman's scales are weighted against herself. She is measuring the impossible. She is measuring the self she does not fully want to be. She does not want to accept the contradictions, nor the beauty. She wishes the other woman would go away. She wishes the other woman would become someone else, anyone other than another Black woman. She has enough trouble dealing with being herself. "Why don't you learn to fly straight," she says to the other woman. "Don't you understand what your poor showing says about us all? If I could fly I'd certainly do a better job than *that*. Can't you put on a more together show? The white girls do it. Maybe we could get one to show you how." The other woman cannot speak. She is too busy keeping herself from crashing upon the ground. She will not cry the tears which are hardening into little sharp stones that spit from her eyes and implant themselves in the first woman's heart, who quickly heals over them and identifies them as the source of her pain.

V

There are myths of self-protection that hold us separate from each other and breed harshness and cruelty where we most need softness and understanding.

1. That courtesy or politeness require our not noticing each other directly, only with the most covert of evaluating glances. At all costs, we must avoid the image of our fear. "How beautiful your mouth is" might well be heard as "Look at those big lips." We maintain a discreet distance between each other also because that distance between us makes me less you, makes you less me.

When there is no connection at all between people, then anger is a way of bringing them closer together, of making contact. But when there is a great deal of connectedness that is problematic or threatening or unacknowledged, then anger is a way of keeping people separate, of putting distance between us.

2. That because we sometimes rise to each other's defense against outsiders, we do not need to look at devaluation and dismissal among ourselves. Support against outsiders is very different from cherishing each other. Often it is a case of "like needs like." It doesn't mean we have to appreciate that *like* or our need of it, even when that *like* is the only thin line between dying and living.

For if I take the white world's estimation of me as Black-woman-synonymous-with-garbage to heart, then deep down inside myself I will always believe that I am truly good for nothing. But it is very hard to look absorbed hatred in the face. It is easier to see you as good for nothing because you are like me. So when you support me because you are like me, that merely confirms that you are nothing too, just like me. It's a no-win position, a case of nothing supporting nothing and someone's gonna have to pay for that one, and it sure ain't gonna be me! When I can recognize my worth, I can recognize yours.

3. That perfection is possible, a correct expectation from ourselves and each other, and the only terms of acceptance, humanness. (Note how very useful that makes us to the external institutions!) If you are like me, then you will have to be a lot better than I am in order to even be good enough. And you can't be because no matter how good you are you're still a Black woman, just like me. (Who does she think she is?) So any act or idea that I could accept or at least examine from anyone else is not even tolerable if it comes from you, my mirror image. If you are not THEIR image of perfection, and you can't ever be because you are a Black woman, then you are a reflection upon me. We are never good enough for each other. All your faults become magnified reflections of my own threatening inadequacies. I must attack you first before our enemies confuse us with each other. But they will anyway.

Oh mother, why were we armed to fight with cloud-wreathed swords and javelins of dust? "Just who do you think you are, anyway?" Who I am most afraid of (never) meeting.

VI

The language by which we have been taught to dismiss ourselves and our feelings as suspect is the same language we use to dismiss and suspect each other. Too pretty — too ugly. Too Black — too white. Wrong. I already know that. Who says so. You're too questionable for me to hear you. You speak THEIR language. You don't speak THEIR language. Who do you think you are? You think you're better than anybody else? Get out of my face.

We refuse to give up the artificial distances between us, or to examine our real differences for creative exchange. I'm too different for us to communicate. Meaning, I must establish myself as not-you. And the road to anger is paved with our unexpressed fear of each other's judgment. We have not been allowed to experience each other freely as Black women in america; we come to each other coated in myths, stereotypes, and expectations from the outside, definitions not our own. "You are my reference group, but I have never worked with you." How are you judging me? As Black as you? Blacker than you? Not Black enough? Whichever, I am going to be found wanting in some way . . .

We are Black women, defined as never-good-enough. I must overcome that by becoming better than you. If I expect enough from myself, then maybe I can become different from what they say we are, different from you. If I become different enough, then maybe I won't be a "nigger bitch" anymore. If I make you different enough from me, then I won't need you so much. I will become strong, the best, excel in everything, become the very best because I don't dare to be anything else. It is my only chance to become good enough to become human.

If I am myself, then you cannot accept me. But if you can accept me, that means I am what you would like to be, and then I'm not "the real thing." But then neither are you. WILL THE REAL BLACK WOMAN PLEASE STAND UP?

We cherish our guilty secret, buried under exquisite clothing and expensive makeup and bleaching creams (yes, still!) and hair straighteners masquerading as permanent waves. The killer instinct toward any one of us who deviates from the proscribed cover is precise and deadly.

Acting like an insider and feeling like the outsider, preserving our self-rejection as Black women at the same time as we're getting over — we think. And political work will not save our souls, no matter how correct and necessary that work is. Yet it is true that without political work we cannot hope to survive long enough to effect any change. And self-empowerment is the most deeply political work there is, and the most difficult.

When we do not attempt to name the confusion of feelings which exist between sisters, we act them out in hundreds of hurtful and unproductive ways. Never speaking from the old pain, to beyond. As if we have made a secret pact between ourselves not to speak, for the expression of that unexamined pain might be accompanied by other ancient and unexpressed hurtings embedded in the stored-up anger we have not expressed. And that anger, as we know from our flayed egos of childhood, is armed with a powerful cruelty learned in the bleakness of too-early battles for survival. "You can't take it, huh!" The Dozens. A Black game of supposedly friendly rivalry and name-calling; in reality, a crucial exercise in learning how to absorb verbal abuse without faltering.

A piece of the price we paid for learning survival was our childhood. We were never allowed to be children. It is the right of children to be able to play at living for a little while, but for a Black child, every act can have deadly serious consequences, and for a Black girl child, even more so. Ask the ghosts of the four little Black girls blown up in Birmingham. Ask Angel Lenair, or Latonya Wilson, or Cynthia Montgomery, the three girl victims in the infamous Atlanta murders, none of whose deaths have ever been solved.

Sometimes it feels as if I were to experience all the collective hatred that I have had directed at me as a Black woman, admit its implications into my consciousness, I might die of the bleak and horrible weight. Is that why a sister once said to me, "white people feel, Black people do"?

It is true that in america white people, by and large, have more time and space to afford the luxury of scrutinizing their emotions. Black people in this country have always had to attend closely to the hard and continuous work of survival in the most material and immediate planes. But it is a temptation to move from this fact to the belief that Black people do not need to examine our feelings; or that they are unimportant, since they have so often been used to stereotype and infantalize us; or that these feelings are not vital to our survival; or, worse, that there is some acquired virtue in not feeling them deeply. That is carrying a timebomb wired to our emotions.

There is a distinction I am beginning to make in my living between *pain* and *suffering*. Pain is an event, an experience that must be recognized, named, and then used in some way in order for the experience to change, to be transformed into something else, strength or knowledge or action.

Suffering, on the other hand, is the nightmare reliving of unscrutinized and unmetabolized pain. When I live through pain without recognizing it, self-consciously, I rob myself of the power that can come from *using* that pain, the power to fuel some movement beyond it. I condemn myself to reliving that pain over and over and over whenever something close triggers it. And that is suffering, a seemingly inescapable cycle.

And true, experiencing old pain sometimes feels like hurling myself full force against a concrete wall. But I remind myself that I HAVE LIVED THROUGH IT ALL ALREADY, AND SURVIVED.

Sometimes the anger that lies between Black women is not examined because we spend so much of our substance having to examine others constantly in the name of self-protection and survival, and we cannot reserve enough energy to scrutinize ourselves. Sometimes we don't do it because the anger's been there so long we don't know what it is, or we think it's natural to suffer rather than to experience pain. Sometimes, because we are afraid of what we will find. Sometimes, because we don't think we deserve it.

The revulsion on the woman's face in the subway as she moves her coat away and I think she is seeing a roach. But I see the hatred in her eyes because she wants me to see the hatred in her eyes, because she wants me to know in only the way a child can know that I don't belong alive in her world. If I'd been grown, I'd probably have laughed or snarled or been hurt, seen it for what it was. But I am five years old. I see it, I record it, I do not name it, so the experience is incomplete. It is not pain; it becomes suffering.

And how can I tell you I don't like the way you cut your eyes at me if I know that I am going to release all the unnamed angers within you spawned by the hatred you have suffered and never felt?

So we are drawn to each other but wary, demanding the instant perfection we would never expect from our enemies. But it is possible to break through this inherited agony, to refuse acquiescence in this bitter charade of isolation and anger and pain.

I read this question many times in the letters of Black women, "Why do I feel myself to be such an anathema, so isolated?" I hear it spoken over and over again, in endless covert ways. But we can change that scenario. We can learn to mother ourselves.

What does that mean for Black women? It means we must establish authority over our own definition, provide an attentive concern and expectation of growth which is the beginning of that acceptance we came to expect only from our mothers. It means that I affirm my own worth by committing myself to my own survival, in my own self and in the self of other Black women. On the other hand, it means that as I learn my worth and genuine possibility, I refuse to settle for anything less than a rigorous pursuit of the possible in myself, at the same time making a distinction between what is possible and what the outside world drives me to do in order to prove I am human. It means being able to recognize my successes, and to be tender with myself, even when I fail.

We will begin to see each other as we dare to begin to see ourselves; we will begin to see ourselves as we begin to see each other, without aggrandizement or dismissal or recriminations, but with patience and understanding for when we do not quite make it, and recognition and appreciation for when we do. Mothering ourselves means learning to love what we have given birth to by giving definition to, learning how to be both kind and demanding in the teeth of failure as well as in the face of success, and not misnaming either.

When you come to respect the character of the time you will not have to cover emptyness with pretense. *

We must recognize and nurture the creative parts of each other without always understanding what will be created.

As we fear each other less and value each other more, we will come to value recognition within each other's eyes as well as within our own, and seek a balance between these visions. Mothering. Claiming some power over who we choose to be, and knowing that such power is relative within the realities of our lives. Yet knowing that only through the use of that power can we effectively change those realities. Mothering means the laying to rest of what is weak, timid, and damaged — without

---

* From *The I Ching.*

despisal — the protection and support of what is useful for survival and change, and our joint explorations of the difference.

I recall a beautiful and intricate sculpture from the court of the Queen Mother of Benin, entitled "The Power Of The Hand." It depicts the Queen Mother, her court women, and her warriors in a circular celebration of the human power to achieve success in practical and material ventures, the ability to make something out of anything. In Dahomey, that power is female.

VIII

Theorizing about self-worth is ineffective. So is pretending. Women can die in agony who have lived with blank and beautiful faces. I can afford to look at myself directly, risk the pain of experiencing who I am not, and learn to savor the sweetness of who I am. I can make friends with all the different pieces of me, liked and disliked. Admit that I am kinder to my neighbor's silly husband most days than I am to myself. I can look into the mirror and learn to love the stormy little Black girl who once longed to be white or anything other than who she was, since all she was ever allowed to be was the sum of the color of her skin and the textures of her hair, the shade of her knees and elbows, and those things were clearly not acceptable as human.

Learning to love ourselves as Black women goes beyond a simplistic insistence that "Black is beautiful." It goes beyond and deeper than a surface appreciation of Black beauty, although that is certainly a good beginning. But if the quest to reclaim ourselves and each other remains there, then we risk another superficial measurement of self, one superimposed upon the old one and almost as damaging, since it pauses at the superficial. Certainly it is no more empowering. And it is empowerment — our strengthening in the service of ourselves and each other, in the service of our work and future — that will be the result of this pursuit.

I have to learn to love myself before I can love you or accept your loving. You have to learn to love yourself before you can love me or accept my loving. Know we are worthy of touch before we can reach out for each other. Not cover that sense of worthlessness with "I don't want you" or "it doesn't matter" or "white folks feel, Black folks DO." And these are enormously difficult to accomplish in an environment that consistently encourages nonlove and cover-up, an environment that warns us to be quiet about our need of each other, by defining our dissatisfactions as unanswerable and our necessities as unobtainable.

Until now, there has been little that taught us how to be kind to each other. To the rest of the world, yes, but not to ourselves. There have been few external examples of how to treat another Black woman with kindness, deference, tenderness or an appreciative smile in passing, just because she IS; an understanding of each other's shortcomings because we have been somewhere close to that, ourselves. When last did you compliment another sister, give recognition to her specialness? We have to consciously study how to be tender with each other until it becomes a habit because what was native has been stolen from us, the love of Black women for each other. But we can practice being gentle with ourselves by being gentle with each other. We can practice being gentle with each other by being gentle with that piece of ourselves that is hardest to hold, by giving more to the brave bruised girlchild within each of us, by expecting a little less from her gargantuan efforts to excel. We can love her in the light as well as in the darkness, quiet her frenzy toward perfection and encourage her attentions toward fulfillment. Maybe then we will come to appreciate more how much she has taught us, and how much she is doing to keep this world revolving toward some livable future.

It would be ridiculous to believe that this process is not lengthy and difficult. It is suicidal to believe it is not possible. As we arm ourselves with ourselves and each other, we can stand toe to toe inside that rigorous loving and begin to speak the impossible — or what has always seemed like the impossible — to one another. The first step toward genuine change. Eventually, if we speak the truth to each other, it will become unavoidable to ourselves.

Grenada Revisited:
An Interim Report*

THE FIRST TIME I came to Grenada I came seeking "home," for this was my mother's birthplace and she had always defined it so for me. Vivid images remained of what I saw there and of what I knew it could become.

• Grand Anse Beach was a busy thoroughfare in the early, direct morning. Children in proper school uniforms carrying shoes, trying to decide between the lure of a coco palm adventure to one side and the delicious morning sea on the other, while they are bound straightforward to well-worn chalky desks.

• The mended hem of the print dress the skinny old woman wore, swinging along down the beach, cutlass in hand. Oversized, high rubber boots never once interfering with her determined step. Her soft shapeless hat. Underneath, sharp, unhurried eyes snapped out from chocolate skin dusted grey with age.

• Another woman, younger, switch held between elbow and waist, driving seven sheep that look like goats except goats carry their tails up and sheep down.

• The Fat-Woman-Who-Fries-Fish-In-The-Market actually did, and it was delicious, served on the counterboards with her

---

* I spent a week in Grenada in late December, 1983, barely two months after the U.S. invasion of the Black Caribbean island my parents left some sixty years earlier. It was my second visit in five years. This is an interim essay, a report written as the rest of Sister Outsider was already being typeset.

fragrant chocolate-tea in mugs fashioned from Campbell's Pork 'n Beans cans with metal handles attached.

• The full moon turning the night beach flash green.

I came to Grenada for the first time eleven months before the March 13, 1979 bloodless coup of the New Jewel Movement which ushered in the People's Revolutionary Government (PRG) of Grenada under Prime Minister Maurice Bishop. This brought an end to twenty-nine years of Sir Eric Gairy's regime – wasteful, corrupt, and United States sanctioned.

The road from tiny Pearl's Airport in Grenville, up over Grand Etang mountain through Beauregard and Birch Grove, a rainbow of children calling after us down the one narrow road through these hamlets cut into the hills. Tree ferns straight up like shingles along the mountainside. In 1978 there was only one paved road in Grenada. During the People's Revolutionary Government, all roads were widened and reworked, and a functioning bus service was established that did more than ferry tourists back and forth to the cruise ships lying at anchor in the careenage. Wild banana fronds, *baligey*, in clumps below the road's slope. Stands of particular trees within the bush – red cocoa fruit, golden apple, mango, breadfruit, peach-ripe nutmeg, banana. Girls on the road to Annandale, baskets of laundry balanced on their heads, hands on hips, swaying, reminiscent of 100 roads through Africa.

Grenada, tiny spice island, is the second largest producer of nutmeg in the world. Its cocoa has a 45 percent fat content and sells for premium prices on the world market. But Grenadians pay eight times more than that price if they wish to drink processed hot chocolate, all of which is imported.

The second time I came to Grenada I came in mourning and fear that this land which I was learning had been savaged, invaded, its people maneuvered into saying thank you to their invaders. I knew the lies and distortions of secrecy surrounding the invasion of Grenada by the United States on October 25, 1983; the rationalizations which collapse under the weight of facts; the facts that are readily available, even now, from the back pages of the *New York Times*.

1. *That the St. Georges Medical School students were in danger.*
Officials of the school deny this.[1] Students deny this.[2] The U.S.
government had received assurances from General Hudson
Austin of the Revolutionary Military Council guaranteeing the
students' safety. These assurances were ignored.[3]

2. *That the U.S. was invited to intervene by the signers of an
Organization of Eastern Caribbean States Treaty.* This would only
have been internationally legal had *Grenada* invaded another
island.[4] The decision to invade was made by four of the seven
signatories. The invitation itself was actually drafted by the
U.S. State Department and sent down to the Eastern Caribbean nations.[5]

3. *That Grenada threatened U.S. security because of the construc-
tion of a military airport and the stockpiling of an arsenal of modern
weapons.* Grenada's new airport is a civilian airport built to ac-
commodate tourists. It has been in planning for over twenty-five
years, half financed by several western european countries and
Canada. According to Plessey, the British firm who underwrote
the project, the airport was being built to civil, not military,
standards.[6] All U.S. reports on Grenada now stress the necessity of this airport for a Grenadian tourist industry.[7] The
"stockpile" of weapons was less than two warehouses. Of 6,300
rifles, about 400 were fairly modern; the rest were very old, and
some antique.[8]

As even Arthur Schlesinger, Jr. observed, "Now we launch a
sneak attack on a pathetic island of 110,000 people with no army, no navy or air force, and claim a glorious victory." [9]

A group of men and women mend the road ahead of us with
hoes and rock hammers, wheelbarrows, and other hand tools.
They step to one side as we pass by. One woman wipes her face
with the end of her headcloth, leaning upon the handle of her
scythe. Another woman is barefooted, young, but when she
smiles I see all of her front teeth are missing. The PRG brought
free medical care to Grenada, and no more school fees. Most
estate workers and peasants in the small villages saw a dentist
for the first time in their lives. Literacy was raised by teacher
education and a planned each-one-teach-one program through
the countryside.

Revolution. A nation decides for itself what it needs. How best to get it. Food. Dentists. Doctors. Roads. When I first visited Grenada in 1978, one-third of the farmable land in the country lay idle, owned by absentee landlords who did not work it. The PRG required that plans be filed either for farming that land, turning it over to those who would, or deeding it to the state. Small banana collectives started. Fishing cooperatives. Beginning agro-industry. The World Bank notes the health of the Grenadian economy, surpassing all other Caribbean economies in the rate of its growth and stability despite the opposition of the U.S. Unemployment dips from 40 percent to 14 percent. Now there is no work again.

Four years ago, the U.S. acted through the International Monetary Fund to assure that there would be no western money available for the Grenadian economy, much less for protecting her shores from an invasion threatened by Gairy operating out of San Diego, California, where he had sought asylum. When the PRG sought economic aid from the U.S. in 1979 to help rebuild the infrastructure of a country fallen into despair during the twenty-nine years of Gairy's regime, the U.S. response was to offer the insult of $5000 from an ambassador's discretionary fund! Now it is 1983, post-invasion, and the conquerors are promising Grenadians welfare, their second main exportable drug. Three million dollars thus far, administered under U.S. guns, so long as the heads that take it are bowed.

Had the amount this invasion cost each one of us in taxes been lent to the PRG when it requested economic aid from the U.S. five years ago, the gratitude of Grenadians would have been real, and hundreds of lives could have been saved. But then Grenada would have been self-defined, independent; and, of course, that could not be allowed. What a bad example, a dangerous precedent, an independent Grenada would be for the peoples of Color in the Caribbean, in Central America, for those of us here in the United States.

The ready acceptance by the majority of americans of the Grenadian invasion and of the shady U.S. involvement in the events leading up to the assassination of Prime Minister Maurice Bishop both happen in an america whose moral and ethical fiber is weakened by racism as thoroughly as wood is weakened by dry rot. White america has been well-schooled in the dehumanization of Black people. A Black island nation? Why, don't be ridiculous! If *they* weren't all so uppity, *we'd* have enough jobs and no recession. The lynching of Black youth and shooting down of Black women, 60 percent of Black teenagers unemployed and rapidly becoming unemployable, the presidential dismantling of the Civil Rights Commission, and more Black families below the poverty line than twenty years ago — if these facts of american life and racism can be passed over as unremarkable, then why not the rape and annexation of tiny Black Grenada?

The Pentagon has been spoiling for a fight it could win for a long time; the last one was the battle for Inchon in the 1950s. How better to wipe out the bitter memories of Vietnam defeats by Yellow people than with a restoration of power in the eyes of the american public — the image of american marines splashing through a little Black blood? ". . . to keep our honor clean" the marine anthem says. So the american public was diverted from recession, unemployment, the debacle in Beirut, from nuclear madness and dying oceans and a growing national depression and despair, by the bombing of a mental hospital where fifty people were killed. Even that piece of proud news was withheld for over a week while various cosmetic stories were constructed. Bread and circuses.

If the United States is even remotely interested in seeing democracy flourish in the Caribbean, why does it continue to support Haiti and the Dominican Republic, two of the most corrupt and repressive governments in the Americas? The racism that coats the U.S. government lies about Grenada is the same racism that blinded american eyes to the Black faces of 131 Haitians washed up on shore in Miami, drowned fleeing the Duvalier regime. It is the same racism that keeps american eyes turned aside from the corrosive apartheid eating like acid into the face of White South Africa and the Reagan government which shares her bed under the guise of "constructive engagement." White South Africa has the highest standard of living of any nation in the world, and 50 percent of Black South Africa's children die before they are five. A statistic. The infant mortality rate for Black americans is almost twice that of white americans — in the most highly industrialized country in the world. White america has been well-schooled in the acceptance of Black destruction. So what is Black Grenada and its 110,000 Black lives?

Unemployment in Grenada dropped 26 percent in four years.[10] On October 25, 1983 american Corsair missiles and naval shells and mortars pounded into the hills behind Grenville, St. Georges, Gouyave. American marines tore through homes and hotels searching for "Cubans." Now the Ministries are silent. The state farms are at a standstill. The cooperatives are suspended. The cannery plant in True Blue is a shambles, shelled to silence. On the day after the invasion, unemployment was back up to 35 percent. A cheap, acquiescent labor pool is the delight of supply side economics. One month later, the U.S. Agency for International Development visits Grenada. They report upon the role of the private sector in Grenada's future, recommending the revision of tax codes to favor private enterprise (usually foreign), the development of a labor code that will ensure a compliant labor movement, and the selling off of public sector enterprises to private interests.[11] How soon will it be Grenadian women who are going blind from assembling microcomputer chips at $.80 an hour for international industrial corporations? "I used to work at the radio station," says a young woman on the beach, shrugging. "But that ended in the war."

This short, undeclared, and cynical war against Grenada is not a new direction for american foreign policy. It is merely a blatant example of a 160-year-old course of action called the Monroe Doctrine. In its name america has invaded small Caribbean and Central American countries over and over again since 1823, cloaking these invasions under a variety of names. Thirty-eight such invasions occurred prior to 1917 before the Soviet Union even existed. For example, in 1897, U.S. marines landed in Puerto Rico to fight the Spanish-American War. They never left.

Beginning in 1981, the United States rehearsed the invasion of Grenada openly. It practiced the war game *Ocean Venture* in which it bombed the Puerto Rican island of Vieques, calling it "Amber of the Amberdines" (Grenada of the Grenadines). In this grisly make-believe, a situation is supposed to occur where americans are held hostage. As we know, this was the first excuse used to justify the invasion of Grenada. As for americans really being in danger, there were still over 500 resident american citizens who chose to remain in Grenada during and after the invasion. But since *Ocean Venture* appears to be the script, we must remember that it also calls for the assassination of the Prime Minister of Amber. Are we now to believe that the U.S./CIA was not involved directly or indirectly with Prime Minister Maurice Bishop's death? Was the coup which served as the opening for *Ocean Venture* to become a reality merely an unhappy coincidence of personal intrigue, or was it an event lengthily orchestrated by clever manipulators?

The Pentagon has admitted in secret Congressional briefings that it knew of the coup against Bishop two weeks before it happened.[12] The Ranger unit participating in the invasion had spent six days between September 23 and October 2, 1983 practicing the takeover of an airport and the liberation of hostages, a maneuver about which the Pentagon had requested no publicity.[13] One Senator disclosed that there were CIA agents accompanying the seventy students flown out of Grenada on October 26, the day after the invasion.[14]

There will be a long and painstaking search for answers to these questions.

P.S.Y.O.P.S., the psychological operations unit of the U.S. occupation forces — a new development heard from in combat here for the first time — was quick to plaster St. Georges and the rest of Grenada with posters of Bernard Coard and General Hudson Austin, stripped naked and blindfolded, holding them up to ridicule and scorn as the slayers of the Grenadian people's beloved Maurice Bishop. It is well known that had Bishop lived, Grenada would have fought any invasion down to the last child. So scapegoats for his death were essential. The details of the power struggles which occurred within the New Jewel Movement Party — if such they were — are yet to be known and assuredly complex. Yet months later, these men are still being held incommunicado in Richmond Hill prison, St. Georges, by "security forces," non-Grenadian. They have not been charged nor brought to trial as of this writing, nor have the forty-odd other Grenadians still detained with them.

Nothing is now heard of the two americans known to have been involved in the last days of the Bishop regime, one of whom was wanted on a weapons charge here in the U.S., and one of whom holds passports in two countries.[15] Who were they working for and on what side? Their identities have never been divulged — a favorite tactic to cover destabilization operatives — and their existence attested to only by one line in the back pages of the *New York Times*. So, too, was the assertion by Ambassador to France Evan Galbraith on public TV that the U.S. was involved in Grenada "weeks before Bishop's death."[16]

A West German nurse working in Grenada, Regina Fuchs, reports she was jailed and relentlessly interrogated after being falsely accused of harboring fugitives by two americans, one of whom, Frank Gonzales, identified himself to her as CIA.[17]

The action in Grenada served many purposes for the United States, provided the grounds for many tests. A major one was addressed to the concern long expressed by the Pentagon as to whether or not Black american soldiers could be gotten to fire upon other Black people. This becomes a vital question as the U.S. military-industrial complex executes increasingly military solutions to this country's precarious position in the Third World, where the U.S. either ignores or stands upon the wrong side of virtually every single struggle for liberation by oppressed peoples. Of course, there were also lesser tests. In addition to trying out new armaments, there was the question of whether the marines liked their new Nazi-style helmets. They did not because they couldn't shave in them. And whether the new army uniforms were too heavy to be worn comfortably in the tropics. They were.[18]

Listen to the language that came from the Pentagon, orchestrated by the psychological warfare experts operating in Grenada.

- *We got there just in time.*
- *Not an invasion, a rescue mission.*
- *Mopping up.*
- *It was our turf. We had every right.*
- *Armed thugs* (the Grenadian militia).
- *An Idi Amin-type character, capable of taking hostages* (General Austin.)
- *Imprisoned for spreading ill will among the people.*

This language is calculated to reduce a Black nation's aspirations in the eyes and ears of white americans already secretly terrified by the Black Menace, enraged by myths of Black Progress, at the same time encouraged by government action never to take the life of a Black person seriously.

Even many Black americans, threatened by some spectre of a socialism that is mythic and undefined at best, have bought the government line of "them" against "us." But which one of us as a Black american has ever taken the time to examine this threat of socialism for any reality nearly as destructive as racism is within all of our lives? With the constant manipulation of the media, many Black americans are honestly confused, defending "our" invasion of Black Grenada under a mistaken mirage of patriotism.

Nineteen eighty-four is upon us, and doublethink has come home to scramble our brains and blanket our protest.

In addition to being a demonstration to the Caribbean community of what will happen to any country that dares to assume responsibility for its own destiny, the invasion of Grenada also serves as a naked warning to thirty million African-americans. Watch your step. We did it to them down there and we will not hesitate to do it to you. Internment camps. Interrogation booths. Isolation cells hastily built by U.S. occupation forces. Blindfolded stripped prisoners. House-to-house searches for phantom Cubans. Neighbors pressured to inform against each other. No strange gods before us. U.S. soldiers at roadblocks and airports, assisted by former members of Gairy's infamous Mongoose Gang, carrying notebooks with lists of Bishop and PRG sympathizers.[19] The tactics for quelling a conquered people. No courts, no charges, no legal process. Welfare, but no reparation for damaged businesses, destroyed homes and lives. Street passes. Imprisonment of "trouble-makers." The new radio station blaring The Beach Boys rock group music hour after hour.

Whose country was Grenada?

Hundreds of Grenadian bodies are buried in unmarked graves, relatives missing and unaccounted for, survivors stunned and frightened into silence by fear of being jailed and accused of "spreading unrest among the people." No recognition and therefore no aid for the sisters, mothers, wives, children of the dead, families disrupted and lives vandalized by the conscious brutality of a planned, undeclared war. No attention given to the Grenadian bodies shipped back and forth across the sea in plastic bodybags from Barbados to Grenada to Cuba and back again to Grenada. After all, they all look alike, and besides, maybe if they are flown around the world long enough they will simply disappear, or become invisible, or some other peoples' sacrifice.

"My brother died in Calliste when they shot up the house," Isme said, "because they thought Cubans were living there. My father lost his arm and a leg. They took him to hospital in Barbados but he passed away there. His body was brought back to Pearl's Airport but I've got to borrow some money now to bring him home for his funeral."

Weeks after the invasion, Grenadians were still smelling out and burying bodies which lay all over the island. The true casualty figures will never be known. No civilian body count is available. Even the bodies of Maurice Bishop and his slain ministers are never positively identified, no doubt to forestall any possible enshrinement by the people who loved him, no doubt to make the task of smearing his popular memory more easily accomplished. It has already begun.

For the first time in an american war, the american press was kept out until the stage could be set. This extends by precedent the meaning of military censorship in this country. At the time, it also deflected attention from the invasion itself. Mission accomplished with "surgical precision" meant attempting to conceal the bombing and destruction of civilian homes, the destruction of a hospital and a radio station and police headquarters; attempting to conceal the american heavy transports left mangled on the side of the road by soldiers not trained to drive to the left, and the civilian cars those army vehicles collided with. It meant the appropriation, use, and destruction of homes and stores and other businesses with no compensation. When the american press was finally admitted after the cosmetic cleanup, we were treated to photographs of smiling Grenadians welcoming their conquerors (look what your tax dollars have bought). But no photos of the signs calling for information about neighbors. No photos of the signs throughout the countryside calling for an end to yankee imperialism. *NO BISHOP NO REVO.*

So what did Revolution in Grenada mean? It meant the inauguration of an agro-industry which for the first time in the island's history processed the island's own fruit, its own coffee, under its own brand, Spice Isle Foods. Canned products from their own soil available in stores. The beginning of a fishing and fish-processing industry. In a country rich with tropical fruit, whose waters abound with fish, why should the most common fruit juice be Florida orange juice, the most commonly used fish, imported saltfish from Canada?

It meant almost doubling the number of doctors on the island from twenty-three to forty, a health center set up in every parish for the first time, a dental clinic. It meant a public health anti-mosquito cleanup campaign implemented by the National Youth Organization that successfully protected Grenada from the wave of Dengue Fever sweeping through the rest of the Caribbean in the summer of 1981.[20]

It meant twelve-year-old Lyndon Adams of L'Esterre, Carriacou, teaching a seventy-three-year-old woman how to read and write as part of the each-one-teach-one program against functional illiteracy conducted by the Center for Popular Education. This highly successful program enlisted the aid of one of the most brilliant educators of all time, Paulo Friere, head of the World Council of Churches' literacy program. When the echos of *Ocean Venture* drifted across the Caribbean from Vieques in 1981, and the stench of the threat of U.S. invasion hung over the hills from Grand Etang to Harvey Vale, Lyndon, one of the youngest teachers in the CPE program, was quoted as saying: "Before the revolution we were not in the light. I will never give up. I rather they kill me dead than I go work for them if they come to take over we land and try to oppress we again." His seventy-three-year-old neighbor and student says: "In L'Esterre now, I find things is plenty better and getting better still. And look how the children developing and doing good! For that boy's age I find he was doing all right!" [21]

The american medical student who witnessed the shooting of the first american marine killed landing on Grenada resists the prompting of her TV interviewer. *Pockets of foreign resistance. Cubans hiding in the hills.* "Oh no, he wasn't shot by Cubans. It was an old man and his son, firing from their house." Lyndon Adams and his neighbor are not Cuban. The old man and his son defending their home were not Cubans. They were Grenadians who dared to believe that they could have a right to define themselves and the future of their nation independent of the United States.

Grenada is a highly stratified society made up of a large, extremely poor mass of estate workers and small land-holding peasants, a small but growing group of urban service workers, and a tiny well-to-do middle class, civil servants and landed, who traditionally have involved themselves with the economics of import-export rather than the economics of national production. The Bishop government was becoming a successful bridge between these different groups. Problems of colorism and classism are deep, far-reaching, and very complex legacies left from successive colonialisms. Grenadians, rightly so, are highly resistant to any external suggestions of a superficial solution. By bringing the goals of these diverse groups together, the Revolution became even more threatening to the U.S.

To the average Grenadian, the United States is a large but dim presence where some dear relative now lives. Until the information campaigns of the PRG, the lack of international news coverage and commentary kept Grenadians largely unaware of the U.S. position in world politics and its history of institutionalized racism and classism. Ronald Reagan was seen as a fatherly movie star unconnected to policies of systematic economic and military oppression of people of Color throughout the developing countries of the world.

But the average Grenadian is also extremely involved with the political affairs of his and her own country, wherever there is room beyond survival concerns for such involvement. Facets of the October events surface in every conversation, guarded or unguarded, casual or otherwise.

The conflicts in the New Jewel Movement, Bishop's house arrest, the subsequent demonstration of ten thousand Grenadians, the second smaller march which resulted in Bishop's liberation and murder along with other Ministers and hundreds of Grenadians on Richmond Hill, and the four-day military curfew that followed these events left terror in the hearts of all Grenadians. Any ending seemed preferable at the time.

The U.S.-operated Spice Island Radio went into operation the afternoon of the invasion, and most Grenadians obtained whatever information they got about events from posters and handbills put up around the countryside by P.S.Y.O.P.S. Rumors have been rife among the people, attempting to explain the inexplicable. One shopgirl in St. Georges told me she had heard the reason why the army fired upon the people at Fort Rupert was because "the Russians had put tablets into their milk that would make them shoot anybody on sight."

It remains to be seen if the future plans of the U.S. for Grenada will justify the vision of many Grenadians of the United States as savior. Even now this view is not nearly as widespread as the american media would have us believe. Says a newly unemployed nineteen-year-old laborer in St. Georges, "They can call it a rescue mission all they want, but I haven't been rescued yet." There is much pain beneath the veneer of gratitude: too many fathers and uncles and brothers and daughters injured and killed because "the americans thought there were Cubans living in there." All over Grenada I felt the deadening effect of horror and disbelief in every conversation about the war, often beneath a surface animation.

I came to Grenada my second time six weeks after the invasion, wanting to know she was still alive, wanting to examine what my legitimate position as a concerned Grenadian-american was toward the military invasion of this tiny Black nation by the mighty U.S. I looked around me, talked with Grenadians on the street, the shops, the beaches, on porches in the solstice twilight. Grenada is their country. I am only a relative. I must listen long and hard and ponder the implications of what I have heard, or be guilty of the same quick arrogance of the U.S. government in believing there are external solutions to Grenada's future.

I also came for reassurance, to see if Grenada had survived the onslaught of the most powerful nation on earth. She has. Grenada is bruised but very much alive. Grenadians are a warm and resilient people (I hear my mother's voice: "Island women make good wives. Whatever happens, they've seen worse"), and they have survived colonizations before. I am proud to be of stock from the country that mounted the first Black english-speaking People's Revolution in this hemisphere. Much has been terribly lost in Grenada, but not all — not the spirit of the people. *Forward Ever, Backward Never*[22] is more than a mere whistle in the present dark.

Notes

1. P. Tyler, *Washington Post*, October 10, 1983, p. A14.
2. A. Cockburn, *Village Voice*, November 8, 1983, p.11.
3. B.D. Ayers, *New York Times*, October 22, 1983, p. A5 and J. McQuiston, *New York Times*, October 26, 1983, p. A20.
4. Text of Treaty, *New York Times*, October 26, 1983, p. A19.
5. S. Taylor, *New York Times*, October 26, 1983, p. A19.
6. A. Lewis, *New York Times*, November 3, 1983 and A. Cockburn, *Village Voice*, November 8, 1983, p. 10.
7. S. Mydans, *New York Times*, January 15, 1984, p. 9.
8. *Christian Science Monitor*, November 7, 1983.
9. A. Schlesinger, Jr., *Wall Street Journal*, October 26, 1983.
10. C. Sunshine, ed., *Grenada — The Peaceful Revolution* (E.P.I.C.A., Washington, D.C., 1982).
11. C. Sunshine, *The Guardian*, December 28, 1983.
12. E. Ray and B. Schaap, "U.S. Crushes Caribbean Jewel," *Covert Action Bulletin # 20*, Winter 1984, p. 11.

13. Ibid., p. 13.
14. Ibid., p. 5.
15. S. Taylor, *New York Times*, November 6, 1983, p. 20.
16. Ibid.
17. *Washington Post*, November 21, 1983.
18. CBS Evening News, December 18, 1983.
19. *The London Guardian*, November 4, 1983.
20. *Grenada — The Peaceful Revolution*, p. 87.
21. *Carriacou — In the Mainstream of the Revolution* (Fedon Publishers, St. Georges, Grenada, 1982), pp. 54-57.
22. Slogan of the Grenadian Revolution

ALSO BY AUDRE LORDE

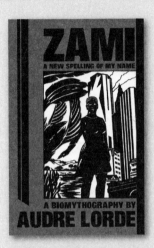

Zami: A New Spelling of My Name
A Biomythography

Zami, a Carriacou name for women who work together as friends and lovers.

> "*Zami* is a fast-moving chronicle. From the author's vivid childhood memories in Harlem to her coming of age in the late 50s, the nature of Audre Lorde's work is cyclical."
> —*Off Our Backs*

> "Filled with finely distilled reflection, as sage and resonant as ancient wisdom literature."
> —*Ms*. magazine

110,000 COPIES SOLD
6 x 9 inches, 256 pages
ISBN-13: 978-0-89584-122-0
ISBN-10: 0-89594-122-8

For a current catalog of books from Crossing Press
visit our Web site: **www.tenspeed.com**